MODERN V
A tutorial for n
By Sam W Wright
Copyright © 2021 All rights
ISBN: 9798506701576

DISCLAIMER

The opinions expressed in this book are those of the author or persons quoted by the author. This book is for information and entertainment purposes. It does not constitute legal or financial advice and should not be used for that purpose. Always consult a licensed professional to determine what is best for your individual circumstances. Your use of the information in this book is at your own risk. As used in this book, the term "wife" can refer to any woman that a man is legally married to; engaged to be married to; considers to be his exclusive girlfriend; cohabits with; has a child with; or provides any financial or emotional support to. The terms man, men, woman, women, he, she, his and hers are biological reference. This book does not recognize or acknowledge modern social / cultural constructs of self-determined gender identity or gender fluidity.

WISE WORDS

". . . I find more bitter than death the woman, whose heart is snares and nets, and her hands as bands: whoso pleaseth God shall escape from her; but the sinner shall be taken by her." ~ Ecclesiastes 7:26 KJV, King Solomon, circa 935 BC

"Give not thy strength unto women, nor thy ways to that which destroyeth kings." ~ c 930 BC Proverbs 31:3, KJV, the words of King Lemuel, which his mother taught him.

"It is better for you to have put your manhood in the mouth of a venomous snake or a pit of burning charcoal than a woman." ~ Gautama Buddha, circa 480 – 400 BC, to a young disciple who broke his vow of celibacy.

"It is better to dwell in the wilderness, than with a contentious and an angry woman." ~ Proverbs 25:24 NASB, King Solomon.

"Second only to Satan and his demonic minions, modern women are the most malevolent and destructive force on earth." ~ Sam W. Wright, 2018, in response to a young man seeking advise about relationships with women.

FOREWORD

The purpose of this book is to help the millions of modern men who have been psychologically and emotionally emasculated by decades of unrelenting abuse by feminized governmental, cultural, social and corporate institutions. This book is not a scientific or theological discourse. It is propositional and based on more than fifty years of professional and personal experience and observation. I include numerous anecdotes in the pages that follow. The names and minor details in those anecdotes were changed to protect the identity of clients, innocent citizens, and former coworkers. But the events described in those anecdotes are essentially true.

Women will angrily deny my propositions and call me a misogynist. For the record, I do not hate women. I do not hate cobras either. But I know what a cobra is, and I know what the likely outcome will be if a man brings one into his home, his business, or his bed. I admit that many women today provide a wide variety of beneficial services to society at large. But bringing peace and contentment into a man's life are not among those services. The statistics speak for themselves.

My views are not new or unique. Enlightened sages have expressed similar views for thousands of years. But you rarely hear what those sages had to say on the subject because modern social and cultural forces ignore them or suppress them. I quote some of those sages at various places in this work. If the sage spoke or wrote in another language, I include what I believe to be the best English translation. Some of those sages are secular. Some are religious. The wisdom offered by any particular sage is valid in spite of his or her human imperfections and regardless of the sacred or secular context in which it originally appeared.

Finally, if you're a man, I am not telling you "Don't get married!" or "Don't date!" I'm just warning you of the likely consequences if you do. Open your eyes. Open your ears. Look at history. Look and the statistics. And listen to the horror stories of the divorced and miserably married men all around you. It might save your life.

THEN AND NOW

Life for mankind has always been difficult. In the mid 1800's the average human life expectancy was around forty years. Men were farmers, ranchers, lumberjacks, miners, cowboys, carpenters, blacksmiths, soldiers, etc. A man's primary tools were his muscles and his brain. He had to construct his own shelter, grow crops and hunt game using primitive tools and weapons.

Those endeavors were beyond the physical abilities of a woman. She needed a man to help her survive. And a man, physically and emotionally exhausted by labor and loneliness, needed a woman to make his life more bearable. A man's natural physical and psychological superiority gave him an advantage. Women knew that, and they respected it. So the two of them married and built a life together, albeit a relatively short one. While he did the dangerous hard labor, she showed her appreciation by washing and mending his clothes, preparing his meals, cleaning his home, and sharing his bed. And it took both of them to turn their savage offspring into semi-civilized adults. When the sun went down, oil lamps or candles provided just enough light for them to prepare for the next day before going to bed. And they were up the next day before the sun. Anyone who stayed in bed beyond that was ill or dead. That hard life, and working together for each other's well-being forged bonds of mutual appreciation and love. And when one of them inevitably died, the surviving mate's sense of loss was genuine.

As the industrial revolution gained momentum, men built machines and made scientific discoveries that expanded their productivity many times and increased the average human life expectancy by decades. Electricity, lights, telephones, indoor plumbing, washing machines, dryers, dishwashers, vacuum cleaners, and a host of other inventions made the lives of women much easier and gave them more leisure time than they had ever known.

Fast forward to twenty-first century America. Life is still more dangerous and difficult for men than for women. Men are the block masons, roofers, miners, longshoremen, iron workers, carpenters, oil and gas rig roustabouts, heavy equipment operators, utility line workers, commercial fishermen, military combat specialists, etc. The few women who arrogantly venture into those professions don't last long, and they often create additional danger and labor for the men who have to work with them. In addition to doing their own jobs, men often have to rescue or clean up after the women they are forced to work with. But when men politely suggest that women would be happier and more useful if they spent their time and energy improving their physical, mental, and spiritual health, and doing jobs that they are more physically and psychologically suited for, women reply with a fusillade of vicious personal insults.

Modern women treat the world as their toilet. They treat men as excrement. They have pointed their collective middle finger toward heaven and have ordained themselves high priestesses. Their religion is narcissism. Their sacred scripture is "Cosmo." Their vestments are Haute Couture. Their temples are spas and salons. Their communion elements are anti-depressants and alcohol. And their god is a mirror. They spend nearly every waking moment worshiping that god, and the fire of their sacrifices to it does not go out until they are dead. And men, to our own everlasting shame, have facilitated this blasphemy by ignoring it or encouraging it, instead of (figuratively speaking, and in keeping with the present metaphor) taking them outside the proverbial gates and stoning them to death.

THE GIRL OF YOUR DREAMS

You're a young man and you think you have found "The girl of your dreams." So you want to marry her before she gets away. Not so fast! Many married men who are older than you thought the same way at one time. They actually married the girl of their dreams, only to discover later that she was a hellish nightmare. Welcome to reality. There are some good women out there. I've occasionally met a few of them. But those women are so few and far between that the odds of you finding one of them is about the same as being struck by lightning. If you think you have found one, it will be nearly impossible for you to tell if she is the genuine article or a spiritual vampire who is planning to suck the life force out of you while emptying your bank account. And if she is the genuine article when you marry her, she probably won't be when she divorces you. It is more likely that she will be a fat argumentative bi-polar shrew, and you will wish that you had been struck by lightning instead.

We all change as we age. But women change more rapidly, more dramatically, and much more disagreeably than men. If you doubt that, you won't have to look far for evidence. Look at your own mother. If that doesn't convince you, look at the mothers of your friends, classmates, and coworkers. If you're still in doubt, look at the morbidly depressed expression on the faces of the men who are or were married to those women. If you think you're some special stud who can dodge that bullet, you're fooling yourself.

CONNECTING THE DOTS

I answered hundreds of domestic disturbance complaints during my decades as a law enforcement officer. During the overlapping three decades as a private investigator and private investigation agency owner, I investigated countless infidelity and child custody cases. About half of my clients in those cases are men. Every week I review the family court filings posted on the court clerk websites of the counties where I do most of my business. About seventy percent of the petitioners in those filings are women. When I read the news, I regularly see stories of men arrested for allegedly battering their wives, or for injuring or killing other men in disputes over women. Then there is the recent spate of women who claim they were sexually assaulted years ago and did not report it at the time, but now demand that their alleged attacker be prosecuted (or rather persecuted) based on their word alone, without due process and without physical evidence.

On top of all this, there are the hundreds of married and divorced men that I have informally interviewed during the past three decades. When I ask those men if they would remarry if they suddenly became single, or if they would marry the first time if they had their lives to live over again, the overwhelming majority of those men answer "No!", or sometimes "Hell No!", and occasionally "No Fucking Way!" When asked why they felt so negatively about marriage, nearly all of them described wives or ex-wives who display behavior patterns that match the psychiatric profession's description of symptoms associated with narcissistic or antisocial personality disorders. Here are some of those symptoms:

- an exaggerated sense of self-importance a sense of entitlement
- requires excessive admiration
- is preoccupied with fantasies about beauty, power, etc
- takes advantage of others to get what they want
- is unwilling to recognize the needs and feelings of others
- is arrogant or haughty
- is impatient or angry when they don't get their way
- has difficulty regulating emotions and behavior
- has difficulty dealing with stress and adapting to change

- is depressed and moody
- is deceitful as indicated by repeated lying
- is impulsive or fails to plan ahead
- is irritable and aggressive
- has disregard for the safety of self or others
- is consistently irresponsible
- has a lack of remorse or rationalizes having hurt others

Sound like any women you know? Of course it does! Probably most of them! So why do the men who are married to these venomous gorgons continue to live in that virtual hell-on-earth instead of just bailing out? Some of them said the cost of divorce would force them into bankruptcy. Others said they were enduring it for the sake of their kids. But one of them gave an answer that captured an underlying sentiment expressed by many of them:

"Personal honor. I vowed to God that I would take her for better or for worse, till death us do part. I took that vow seriously, even if she did not. I love my kids; but if I had seen what a horrible human being was hiding behind her makeup and wedding veil, I wouldn't even have talked to her, let alone married her or had sex with her. Most of my married buddies feel the same way about their wives. About the only good thing she has done for me is taken away my fear of death."

When I share that remark with other married or divorced men, a surprising majority of them agree, at least in part. And yet many less experienced men today still operate under the delusion that there is a "special someone" out there just for them, not realizing that most of those special someones should be under the supervision of a psychiatrist, a prison guard, a probation officer, or a zoo keeper.

Why do young men today not realize that getting married is like playing Russian Roulette with a loaded auto-pistol and hoping for a misfire? I think the answer is two-fold:

1. When they were boys, they had no adult male mentors to teach them the truth about the power and danger of their natural biological impulses and the degree to which modern social, cultural and corporate forces manipulate those impulses for the sake of psychological control and financial gain. By the time those boys became young men, they were conditioned to spend most of their time and energy trying to gratify those impulses instead of learning how to master them.

2. Men today do not see how deep the river

of female malevolence and treachery is, or how swift and powerful its currents. So they try to navigate that river in what amounts to a leaky boat with no motor, no oars, no rudder, no radio, no charts, no first aid kit, and no flotation devices. When that boat goes over the inevitable waterfall, most of the men who survive the crash will crawl back to the river's head, hop into another leaky boat and start down the river again. Insanity truly is doing the same thing over and over again and expecting different results.

The landscape of recent American history is littered with the ruined lives and reputations of seemingly intelligent men who allowed their undisciplined impulses too be exploited by opportunistic parasitic women who were trained and supported by pernicious diabolical forces. Search the internet for successful wealthy male celebrities in politics, sports, show business and religion who lost their jobs, their reputations, their fortunes, and sometimes their liberty, just because they allowed their impulses to guide their interactions with women. Follow their example and you can expect the same results.

Contrary to what has been drummed into your head since birth, you are not a Darwinian animal at the mercy of some unconquerable biological imperative. You are a man with the power of rational thought and the ability to master your impulses if you choose to. Granted, it takes constant vigilance and self-discipline. But mastering those impulses has a higher earthly payoff than any other endeavor you could choose.

What's the payoff? If you're a single young man, spend a few minutes thinking about your personal and professional dreams. Do you think a wife will help you achieve those dreams? And if she does, do you think it will be because she loves you and knows how important those dreams are to your psychological well-being? Or do you think maybe it's because of the goodies she is planning to extract from your success for her own benefit before she dumps you for someone higher on the food chain?

If you're an older man who has been married for a long time, or is now divorced after a long marriage, think about how many of your personal and professional dreams went up in smoke because your wife or ex-wife set them on fire. The motorcycle you didn't get. The business you didn't start. The boat you didn't get. The hobbies you gave up. The friends you lost. The novel you didn't write. The places you didn't visit. And a hundred other things you either didn't do or you gave up because you poured your life into trying to please a woman who was never satisfied; who criticized you, ignored you, cheated on you, lied to you, and eventually abandoned you when you no longer had the capital in your physical and emotional bank accounts to cover her massive daily withdrawals from them. How many times did you patiently accommodate her capricious change of mind? How many times did you silently endure her subtle sarcasm? How many times did you leave your house or hide in your man-cave just to escape her chronic nagging? How many times did you work late so you wouldn't have to listen to her incessant whining? How many times did you drink yourself into a drunken stupor to deaden the pain of her unrelenting passive-aggression? How many times, even if only for a brief moment, did you seriously consider sticking a loaded gun in your mouth and pulling the trigger just to have some peace?

If you are an idealistic young man who thinks I exaggerate, do yourself a favor and talk to some of the men I just described. They're all around you and easy to find. Just look for a guy with prematurely gray hair, premature facial wrinkles, slumped shoulders, a painful shuffling gait, and the sad expression of a man who has given up on life. Or look for a man who has a good paying job, but is living in his car or in a crappy apartment because his wife divorced him and is living comfortably on his court-ordered monthly child support and alimony payments.

A BRAVE NEW WORLD

- Granddaughter Charged In Slaying of Grandparents.
- Bitter mother, 39, is guilty of asking three different men to murder her ex-husband after he won custody of their teenage daughter.
- Mom, 27, tortured and caged her five-year-old daughter before her body was found buried near a landfill site.
- Stepmum accused of slicing genitals off 12-year-old boy with fruit knife in China.
- To hide affair, Telangana woman strangles son. - Russian woman 'strangled lover during rough sex' then 'chopped up the body as part of Satanic ritual'.
- Scottsdale woman accused of shooting boyfriend in genitals.
- Woman caught injecting her son with feces during his cancer treatment sentenced to 7 years. Woman beheaded 11-year-old son as lesbian lover held him down before slicing body parts and barbecuing them.
- Psychologist mom shoots twin daughters to death as they slept before turning the gun on herself, authorities say.

- Las Vegas woman accused of killing daughters because organs 'worth a lot of money'.
- Instagram wannabe 'cut out mother's heart while she was still ALIVE'.
- Georgia babysitter charged with battery, murder of 2-year-old girl.
- Gender studies Ph.D. student accused of stalking, killing ex-boyfriend.
- Texas Mom Abandoned Child at Skating Rink So She Could Smoke Crack.

These are just few of the many stories published about women by legitimate news sources during 2019 and 2020. Some people will say "Not all women are like that!" That is a true statement. But the phrase "Not all women are like that" is an implicit acknowledgment that the majority of them are, even if only to a slightly lesser degree. And most of the people who say "Not all women are like that" are either women who are precisely like that, or pathetic men who are so desperate for female approval that they will do or say anything to get it. Some people will say that many modern men display the same antisocial behaviors as modern women do. That is partially true, but with an important qualification: Most of the men who display those behaviors were raised by single or divorced mothers who taught their sons to think and behave like women; emotionally, irrationally, and selfishly. Furthermore, the number of women who display those behaviors is disproportionately higher than men who display them, and not by a small margin.

Note: Pay particular attention to a woman's "sense of entitlement" in the previous list of personality disorder symptoms. The following anecdote was told to me by a man who worked as an elephant handler for a circus. It is a good metaphorical illustration. He said it was a true story, and I have no reason to doubt him.

When the elephants weren't performing in a show, the "star" elephant (I'll call her "Harriet") was secured by a leg chain in a vacant lot near the main tent. When one of the male circus employees arrived for work each day, he would bring a tasty treat to throw to Harriet as he walked by her. Harriet would start swaying happily as soon as she saw him coming. One day the employee forgot to bring a treat. Harriet began swaying as usual, but the employee passed by without tossing her a treat. Harriet stopped swaying and watched him until he was out of sight. As the employee was leaving at the end of the day, he had to pass by Harriet again.

Harriet saw him coming. She found a broken piece of a concrete block on the ground nearby. As the employee was passing by, Harriet used her trunk to pick up the piece of concrete and sling it at the employee. It struck him in the head and knocked him unconscious.

BE A GENIUS!

"Intellectuals solve problems, geniuses prevent them." - Albert Einstein

Before you make any important decision, you should do a cost versus benefit / return on investment analysis. "Do I really need this? What are the immediate and long term costs? Can I afford it? How will it benefit me? Will it hurt others? Is what I will get in return a fair exchange for what I have to invest? Are there better investment options available? If it has potential negative consequence, do I have resources that will allow me to mitigate the loss and repair the damage?" etc.

Because marriage is potentially the most destructive thing you will do in your life, the first question you should ask yourself when considering it is "Why?" If your answer is "Love", you're delusional. If your answer is "Sex", you're in deep trouble. Or, as comedian Jeff Foxworthy put it: "Getting married for sex is like buying a 747 for the free peanuts." Sex is pleasurable. But the mountains of intolerable bullshit a woman is going to demand that you eat in exchange for granting you occasional access to her rapidly deteriorating body doesn't even come close to being a fair exchange of value; especially when you consider that her personality will deteriorate at two or three times the rate that her body does. By the time most men figure this out, their petite and sweet girlfriends have become their obese and contentious wives. Most married men won't tell you this because they are either too embarrassed to admit their mistake, or they're afraid their wives will find out what they said and make their lives more miserable than they already are, if that's even possible.

A FOOL AND HIS MONEY

If you dreamed of having a new sports car valued at one-hundred thousand dollars, and I was a car dealer who offered to sell you one of those cars for five thousand dollars, you'd be suspicious. So I put the offer in a legally binding written contract with the following conditions:

- There is no warranty.
- You can't test drive it.
- You can't look under the hood, look at the undercarriage, or look in the trunk.
- You can't see the Carfax (™) report.
- And if you aren't happy after buying it, you can only return it to me. I will refund your five thousand dollars and charge you a ninety-five thousand dollar restocking fee.

You'd sign the contract and give me your five thousand dollars, right? Of course not. You'd say "You're out of your mind!" and you'd walk away. Let me change the scenario a little. If you dreamed of having a beautiful wife, and the woman of your dreams suddenly and inexplicably appeared and told you that she would marry you and love you forever, you'd be suspicious. So she puts the offer in a legally binding written contract with the following conditions (figuratively speaking):

- She has no warranty. (if she breaks down, physically or mentally, you have to pay for the repairs. You can't trade her in, and you can't have a rental or loaner while she is in the shop)
- You can't take her for a test drive, look under her hood, look at her undercarriage, or look in her trunk. (have sex with her, see her without her makeup, see if she is wearing undergarments that alter or conceal her natural figure, or see if she had any surgical alterations.)
- You can't see her 'Shefax report', (make any investigative inquiries through any source concerning her present or past physical health, mental health, medications, relationships, employment, education, civil judgments, criminal arrests, traffic citations, credit history, or current debt.)
- And if you discover after marrying her that she isn't who she represented herself to be, she will grant you a divorce in exchange for half of your current assets,

half of your pension, and half of your before taxes income for the next twenty years as a restocking fee.

You'd say "You're out of your mind!" and you'd walk away, Right? Wrong! If you're like far too many men today, you'd sign the contract in a hormone blinded stupor, give her an expensive diamond, and suffer through an elaborate wedding ceremony. You and your "dream girl" would exchange solemn vows in an ornate sanctuary where an officiating clergyman would say "I now pronounce you man and wife." The two of you would then go on an expensive honeymoon that you pay for, to a place that you don't even like but agreed to go to just to make her happy.

From that moment on, your testosterone and self esteem begin a slow dark journey into the abyss, while your new bride begins a more rapid and much darker metamorphosis similar to that of a butterfly, only in reverse. Whereas a fat grotesque caterpillar destroys a plant by consuming its leaves in order to store the biochemical energy it needs to morph into a beautiful butterfly, your bride will, figuratively speaking, morph from a beautiful butterfly into a fat grotesque caterpillar by consuming the leaves of your life in order to store the emotional and financial energy she needs to morph back into a butterfly after she discards your bankrupted and withered carcass onto a proverbial dung heap. She will then find another desperate idiot, and the previously described life cycle (or rather "death cycle") repeats itself. Some unusually gifted women are able to repeat this metamorphosis two or three times before nature prevents them from morphing back to butterfly. They remain the fat grotesque caterpillar on the outside that they really always were on the inside.

NOT YOUR GIRL, JUST YOUR TURN

You expect your wife or fiancee to be faithful to you, right? After all, that's what she led you to believe she would be when she accepted your proposal and said "I do" at the alter, right? No matter what women say while looking at their engagement ring, or while standing beside you at a marriage alter, they have no concept of fidelity and no fear of divine retribution for lying. Wedding vows from women are nothing more than religious virtue signaling to try to impress other people. This is so well known that the matter is hardly worth rehearsing here. Women want to be perceived as virtuous without producing any fruit associated with virtue. White wedding gowns are a prime example. At one time they were recognized as a symbol of purity and virtue. But modern women who have been ridden more than the Staten Island Ferry still insist upon wearing ostentatious white wedding gowns when they marry. No matter how honest and virtuous they present themselves to be, most women today are as truthful as Pinocchio and as faithful as crack whores. They are also incurably hypergamous.

Hypergamy is the act of marrying a person of a superior class. It can also apply to women who aren't married, but claim to be in committed monogamous relationships. The slang term for hypergamy is "Monkey-Branching." If you ever watch a monkey in a zoo or in the wild as it swings from one branch to another, pay close attention to its eyes and its hands. It's always looking for another branch to swing to, and doesn't let go of the one that it is swinging from until it has a secure grip on the one it is swinging to. A woman is like a monkey. She will never stop looking for a higher branch (a man who is richer, taller, better looking, more popular than you), and she will let go of you the moment she has a firm grip on him.

FLIRTING

In 1961, rock singer Del Shannon (real name Charles Westover) co-wrote and recorded "Runaway." It became a major international hit and is No. 472 on Rolling Stone's list of the 500 Greatest Songs of All Time, compiled in 2010. Del followed-up that hit in 1962 with a lesser known song titled "Little Town Flirt." Both songs are worth listing to. But pay special attention to the lyrics of Little Town Flirt. Sadly, Del took his own life in 1990 at 55 years of age. An online biography says that Del asked a girl to go to the senior prom with him when he was in high school. She accepted his invitation. But, as the prom drew near, she dumped him for another boy. The biography says that Del sank into a deep depression that he seemingly never recovered from and that many of the songs he wrote in his adult life resulted from his feelings of hurt and betrayal.

Flirting goes hand in hand with hypergamy. Women, regardless of their relationship status, never stop flirting with other men, either single or married. That flirting might vary in style and degree from woman to woman, but they never stop. If you're her husband and you confront her about flirting with other men, she will deny it.

She will say something like "Don't be silly!" or "He's just a friend!" You're not being silly, and she's lying through her teeth. What she was doing was testing another man's sexual availability by sending him equivocal signals about her own. If the man responds (and a shameful number of men will), all she has to do is follow his lead. If he doesn't respond, the effort cost her nothing. If you ever see your wife flirting, she is looking for one or more of four things:

- Validation of her juvenile vanity.
- Reassurance that her sexual market value hasn't crashed and burned.
- An orgasm from someone other than you.
- Mules that she can put in her corral, from which she can cull a replacement for you (her current mule) who, after she has emotionally and financially ridden you to death, she will leave to rot where you drop while she rides away on her new mount.

Here are a few flirting anecdotes to illustrate:

Bob was a client. He and his wife Sue were married for over twenty-five years. Sue had a friend, Jane. Jane was divorced and lived alone for over fifteen years. She was the same age as Sue. Jane asked Sue if Bob would do a few handyman jobs for her. Since Jane lived alone and had no man to help her, Sue asked Bob. And Bob, being a nice guy, said "Sure." When Bob arrived at Jane's house, she led him to the room where the work was to be done. As Bob was preparing to hang a mirror, Jane picked up a large painting from a nearby chair. She held it up as she called to Bob. When Bob turned around, Jane was holding up a seductive nude portrait of herself from about thirty-five years earlier. She smiled at Bob and said "This is a painting of me a few years ago." I asked Bob what he did. He said "I was stunned. I just said 'Oh. That's nice.' I turned around, hung the mirror and got the hell out of there as quickly as I could." Bob asked me the question that I suspect he already knew the answer to. "Why would a divorced woman, alone in her house with the husband of one of her girlfriends, go out of her way to show him a nude painting of herself?" I told told him there were three possibilities.

1. She wanted to have sex with him, but wanted him to suggest it.
2. She was cock-teasing him for her own vanity.

3. Sue put her up to it to either test his fidelity or to get him to cheat so she would have a good reason to divorce him.

Bob had no reason to think option #3 applied. He asked me if he should tell Sue about the incident. I told him "Absolutely not!" I explained that Jane had plausible deniability and he had no witnesses. Jane could deny his allegation. Or she could say that he propositioned her, but that she rejected his advances. Or, the ultimate nightmare, she could say that he raped her. In any of those cases, he would lose. In the last case her allegation would be believed in spite of his denials. His reputation, his future, and probably his marriage would be toast. Bob asked me how he should deal with Jane in the future. I told him that he should stay as far away from her as possible, even if that meant he had to leave his own house when she came over to visit Sue..

Dale was another client. Dale and his wife Carol were married for twelve years. Carol and Dale attended a holiday party that Carol's boss gave for his employees. Carol and Dale were seated at a large round table with approximately fourteen other guests. One of those guests was Connie, a married coworker of Carol. The seating arrangement put Dale beside Connie. Carol and

Connie's husband were several seats away from each other on the other side of the table. A large white table cloth concealed the lower extremities of the seated guests. As the guests engaged in small talk, Dale suddenly felt a hand grab his thigh and tightly squeeze it. In describing the event, Dale said "It startled the hell out of me. I snapped my head to the right and Connie was looking me dead in the eye as she squeezed my thigh. She stared at me for a few seconds and then took her hand away and went back to talking to other people as though nothing happened." As Bob had done, Dale asked me if he should tell his wife. I told him "No." I explained that it was a no-win scenario and he should avoid any future contact with Connie. I explained that Connie's behavior was sadly typical of many bored and horny middle-aged women looking for a quick thrill from men other than their husbands. If they can't arrange for intercourse, they'll settle for making out, groping, fondling, fingering, or dry humping. Location is not important. Elevators, stairwells, bathrooms, broom closets, desktops, motor vehicles, or under the cover of a table cloth will do. Dale had a troubled look on his face as he asked "If that woman is typical, what about my own wife?" All I could do was smile and say,

"Yeah. Scary, isn't it?"

Following are a few personal anecdotes on the subject. If while reading these you think that I'm a conceited jerk, you're at least half wrong. I'm not conceited. I never was. In fact I was an insecure introvert into my late twenties. During that time, numerous women, about half of them married, flirted with me in ways that made it unmistakably clear that they wanted to have sex with me. I just walked away. The point of these anecdotes is that most seemingly "virtuous" women are actually libidinous sexual opportunists. Like it or not, the woman you marry will probably become one of those women. If she does, you won't know about it until it's too late and she has financially and emotionally wrecked your life. Knowing this in advance probably won't stop some of you from giving your heart to her. But when she breaks it to pieces, the memory of this warning might ease the pain and help you put the pieces back together; at least the pieces that you can find.

When I was 16, my best friend, "Bob", had a high school girlfriend, "Ann." She was a cute cheerleader. One evening Bob took me and Ann to a party at the house of one of his other friends. When Bob and another guy drove to a store to get some ice, Ann remained at the party. Being a shy introvert, I sat by myself on the front porch. Shortly after Bob drove away, Ann came onto the porch, straddled my lap, and began energetically humping me while licking and kissing my neck and face. When I tried to push her away, she became even more aggressive. It scared me half to death. I jumped up. She fell onto the floor. She just got up, giggled, and went back inside with everyone else. I didn't know what to do, so I said nothing about it to Bob.

About two years later I came home for summer break from school out of state. Bob now had a different girlfriend, "Jodi." She was a year or two younger than Bob and me. Because Bob and I hung out together, Jodi and I became friends. Jodi was so pretty! One day Jodi called me and asked if I could give her a ride home from one of her girlfriend's house because she couldn't get in touch with Bob. She didn't have a driver's license or a car. I had both. I drove to the house and honked my horn. Jodi ran to my car, climbed into the front seat, slid right up against me and said "Hi" as she kissed me on the mouth. She then looped her arms around my right arm and held on tightly with her head on my shoulder as I drove to her house. I was dazed and confused. When I stopped in front of her house, she said "Wait here for a minute" and then disappeared inside her house. Like an idiot, I sat there dumbfounded instead of burning rubber to the end of her street. A minute or two later she returned to her previous position. She was wearing perfume, fresh makeup, and a low-cut fluffy sweater. She gave me directions to drive to a lightly traveled public park. When we arrived, she said "Let's go for a walk." As we walked down a park path, she held my hand tightly. Between her being so pretty, her perfume and the touch of her hand, she owned me. She could have led me to an open doorway that was billowing sulfurous smoke and that had a sign hanging over it that said "Abandon all hope, ye who enter here", and I would have cheerfully followed her inside. Instead, she led me to a bench where we sat and kissed for a few minutes. She became my girlfriend; an inexcusable act of stupidity on my part. It cost me the friendship of one of the best guys I've ever known; a loss I regret to this day. Within two months, Jodi dumped me for another guy.

When I was twenty-one I became a police officer in a town of about 17,000 people. One of the other officers called me at home one evening. He told me that the department's records clerk, "Cindy", had a fight with her boyfriend and needed a place to stay for a day or two until they could get things straightened out. He asked if she could stay at my place. I said "Sure. Send her over." Cindy arrived with a few small travel bags. She thanked me profusely for letting her stay there. I said "No problem." I showed her to a spare bedroom she could use and I returned to my own room. At 10pm that evening I was reading in my bed when I heard a knock at my bedroom door. I said "Come in." Cindy entered, dressed in a very short and very see-through negligee. I asked if everything was alright. She said that she just wanted to thank me again for letting her stay there. She asked if there was anything she could do to repay me. I told her I was glad to help her out and that she didn't need to repay me. She sat on the far edge of my bed and seductively leaned towards me as she asked me a few more questions that gave her a reason to stay in my room longer. She eventually realized I wasn't going to change my mind. She said "Okay, goodnight" as she slowly made her way out.

A few months later, "Don", a detective friend of mine at the same department, began an affair with a single local elementary school teacher, "Betty." Don was married. I warned him about the danger of his affair, but he ignored my warning. His wife found out about his affair. She kicked him out of their house and filed for divorce. He continued the affair. Don and Betty joined me for lunch one day while I was on-duty. Betty was a good looking thirty year-old, and Don adored her. Betty knew that Don and I were good friends. Betty called me at home one evening and asked if she could come over to talk to me about a problem she was having with Don. Being young, stupid, and not suspicious, I said "Sure." When Betty arrived, I invited her in. She was heavily made up, perfumed, and wearing tight black slacks, black pumps, and a white blouse with the top buttons unfastened enough to show some cleavage. She sat down on a sofa as I sat in a nearby chair. She invited me to sit on the sofa beside her. I told her I was comfortable where I was and I asked her what her problem was with Don. She went into a lengthy story about how she loved Don, but that he was insensitive to her deep "emotional needs." I told her that there wasn't much I could do about it and that she should tell Don how she felt. She gave me a long silent stare and then said "You have really pretty eyes." I replied something like "Thanks. Well, it's getting late and I need to get rested for work tomorrow." She appeared surprised. I escorted her to the front door and opened it. As she exited, she stopped in the open doorway and turned to face me. She then said "Can I kiss you?" Duh! What was I supposed to say? I wasn't comfortable with this, but I didn't have the experience or mental clarity to say "Hell no! Get out of her you crazy bitch!" So I said "Yeah, if you want to." She planted a passionate kiss on my mouth while I stood there like a wooden Indian in front of a cigar store. I guess she could tell that nothing was going to happen. So she said "Goodnight" and drove away. She probably thought I was gay.

Three years later I was working midnight shift as a patrolman at another agency. Around midnight I was sitting in my cruiser at the edge of the parking lot of a rural night club. There was a nice breeze, so I had my driver's door open for the fresh air. My dome light was on. I was looking down at my clipboard and was engrossed in writing a report. I suddenly realized that someone was practically on top of me in the open doorway. I grabbed my revolver with my right hand while I leaned away and grabbed the collar of my assailant with my left. I looked toward the open doorway to see who my attacker was. It was a drunken female club patron who said that she wanted to have sex with me. She looked to be about forty-five years-old with some hard miles on her. I pushed her away, but she bounced right back. I pushed her away again with more force and I told her to go back inside the club. She did. I drove away.

Two years later I was doing the lead male role in a romantic musical comedy at a community theater. My leading lady, Tammi, was a cute young married school teacher. Her husband was taking care of their two year-old son at home so she could do the show. One evening after a show, Tammi approached me in the parking lot. She stood very close to me and told me that our romantic interaction on stage had caused her to become very attracted to me. She said she was confused and wanted to explore her feelings for me. Flattered and tempted as I was, I was more nauseated by the thought of her poor trusting husband taking care of their two year-old son at home while his wife was trying to seduce me in a dark parking lot. Nothing happened.

About three years later and a hundred miles away, a similar scenario played out in a different romantic musical. This time my leading lady, Lynn, was the wife of a police officer who I helped train about five years earlier. She was a well educated and very attractive young woman about twenty-seven. After a show one evening, Lynn shyly approached me in the parking lot and told me that she had become very attracted to me. She explained that she and her husband had been having difficulties in their marriage, and that our on stage romance had caused her to fantasize about the possibility of a real off-stage romance with me. I told her that I was flattered and that she was very attractive, but that I would not feel right about having a relationship with a married woman, especially one who was the wife of a police officer that I personally knew, even if they were separated. She said she was embarrassed for approaching me and that she appreciated my respect for her husband. I told her that I understood, that I hoped she and her husband could work things out, and that I would forget our conversation.

About six months later I was working part-time as the evening shift DJ at a small radio station. The music was on automated machines, so I was there alone. There wasn't much for me to do but occasionally press a button or two on the control board, give station identifications, and read two minutes of news at the top of each hour. The commercial sales girl was working late one evening as I was in the middle of a two minute news broadcast. She came up behind me, wrapped her arms around me and began grinding herself against me while licking the back of my neck. I was barely able to finish the news before killing the mike, pushing her off, and saying "What the hell is wrong with you!?" She giggled and said something like. "Come on! It's just the two of us here! We can have a good time." I told her she'd better leave before her boyfriend showed up. She assured me that he was busy elsewhere. I told her that I was busy doing my job and that I wasn't going to risk getting fired. She just laughed and walked out.

About a year later I went to work as a show announcer at a theme park. The park put on several shows each day that featured female dancers in Vegas style costumes. These women were very fit and very pretty. About half of them were also very married. These gals all lived about twenty miles from the park, so there was little chance that their husbands would show up unexpectedly. Occasionally the dancers would stay late for brush-up rehearsals. They would call home and tell their husbands that they had to rehearse late that evening. What they didn't tell their husbands was that, after rehearsal, they were going to party with some of the male performers who had rented rooms at a nearby motel. One of the dancers invited me to party with them. I declined the invitation.

About five years later I was working at

another law enforcement agency. A man and woman who worked with me at that agency were married to each other for about fifteen years. We began discussing a joint business venture for some extra income and we agreed to meet at their apartment one evening for further discussions. I arrived at the apartment at the agreed upon time. The wife answered the door and invited me in. She was an unusually pretty woman. She was wearing very tight light blue jeans, blue pumps, and a silk blouse with the top unfastened just enough to reveal the cleavage in her push-up bra. She was heavily made up and perfumed. She explained that her husband was delayed at the office and was running about an hour late. I said "I'll come back in a while." She insisted that I stay and wait for him. We sat and made small talk while waiting for his arrival. Her attire, body language, eye contact, smile, and tone of voice were an unambiguous invitation for a sexual encounter. I would be lying if I said that I was not momentarily aroused by the possibilities. But personal moral convictions were more important to me, so I didn't explore the possibilities any further. When her husband finally arrived, we conducted our business discussions and I left. I immediately lost my appetite for the business venture.

A few years after that, I was working the evening shift as a patrolman at another police agency. My supervisor was a younger female sergeant who was bi-lingual and native to another country. I went to the station to give her some reports to review. The administrative staff was gone for the day. The other officers working that evening were on patrol. The only other person in the building was a dispatcher. The sergeant and I sat in her office and talked shop for a few minutes. Out of the blue, she asked me a question in her native tongue. I didn't speak that language, but I understood enough of it to have a good idea of what she said. Hoping to make this awkward situation go away, I put a stupid look on my face and told her that I didn't understand her language. Instead of letting it go, she looked me in the eye and repeated it in English: "Do you want to have sex?" I paused, chuckled, and said "I better get back out on patrol" as I walked out.

I don't view these events as a testimonial to my irresistible charm. I view them as a testimonial to the brazenly licentious and treacherous nature of women. Except for the drunken woman in the night club parking lot, none of these women were what you would think of as sluts. They weren't alcoholics or drug users. They were well educated and well spoken women who held responsible jobs. And, up to the point where they threw themselves at me, I had no reason to think of them as anything other than respectable ladies. I have talked with many men who shared similar experiences. If you're an idealistic young man today who yearns for a faithful, loving, trustworthy woman to spend your life with, I have two words of advice for you: "Give up."

DAMAGED GOODS

Modern women are damaged goods and they're proud of it. Randomly search their profiles and pictures on dating websites and social media platforms. From teens to sixties, what you will see are filtered selfies, puckered lips, tattoos, piercings, cleavage, camel toes, butt shots, bikinis, etc. And to add a touch of cognitive dissonance to this blatantly whorish behavior, they post philosophical and biblical quotations that are beyond their intellectual and spiritual capacities to understand. If that isn't bad enough, they tag those quotations with moronic editorial comments that sound like compositions by middle school dropouts. It's positively mind-numbing. A surprising number of these women have college degrees, professional certifications, and good jobs.

Never make the mistake of thinking that a well educated and well spoken woman with a responsible job is a not a potential train wreck. As long as she is getting her way, she can function and communicate within tolerable limits. But the moment she doesn't get her way, either personally or professionally, she will go off the rails. Her damage will manifest itself in panic, anger, crying, cursing, yelling, violence, profanity, promiscuity or some other aberrant behavior until someone else comes along, puts out the fire and puts her derailed cars back on the tracks.

An excellent illustration is the case of Lisa Marie Nowak, born 1963. Nowak was an aeronautical engineer, a US Navy captain, a naval flight officer and test pilot, and a NASA astronaut. She was part of the crew of Space Shuttle Discovery during the STS-121 mission in 2006. She was a 1985 graduate of the United States Naval Academy in Annapolis, Maryland. She flew F/A-18 Hornets and EA-6B Prowlers. She logged over 1,500 hours in over 30 different aircraft and was awarded numerous medals and commendations. I'd call that very impressive. But not as impressive as her 2007 arrest for battering and pepper spraying another female Air Force Captain who was romantically involved with a male astronaut that Nowak had been screwing around with. She was charged with attempted kidnapping, battery, attempted vehicle burglary with battery, and destruction of evidence. In 2009 she entered a guilty plea to felony burglary and misdemeanor battery. She was sentenced to a year's probation. In 2011 she petitioned the court to seal the record of her criminal proceedings. Her petition was granted. If you want to read the bizarre details of that case, Wikipedia has a thorough synopsis of it.

It isn't reasonable to believe that no red flags popped up during any of the psychological evaluations Nowak must have undergone to attain all of the positions that she held. So I have to believe that those flags were ignored because Nowak was a woman and the Air Force and NASA wanted a woman for their aerial and outer space dog and pony show. I wonder how many better qualified male candidates were overlooked in favor of Nowak.

NOT MY FAULT

Personal and professional circumstances have allowed me on many occasion to observe and overhear women socializing with each other. Eventually their conversation turned to trashing their ex or soon to be ex-husbands. When I asked them why they married someone who was as bad as they described, the typical reply was "He changed after we married." I was the wrong person to say that to. Knowing how rarely people change, my investigative curiosity would get the better of me. So I would do background investigations on the women and on the men they were complaining about. In nearly every instance, even if the man was a jerk (and some of them were), his basic character and behavior patterns were the same when she filed for divorce as they were when she married him. I also discovered that, in nearly every instance, the woman in question became dissatisfied with her husband about the same time that another man who had more money or was better looking than her husband became interested in having a relationship with her. (see hypergamy / monkey-branching.) Following are some related anecdotes:

A woman who was divorced for more than

twenty years described her ex-husband as an abusive alcoholic. Of course he was not around to tell his side of the story. She tried to appear classy in her style and demeanor, but her body language, micro-expressions, and occasional slips of the tongue showed a vulgar underside. I did some research and discovered that she was not born into the sophisticated circles she enjoyed being in. She was essentially a hick who was born with good looks and a high degree of natural cunning that enabled her to exploit other people for her own benefit. I saw multiple indicators that she spent her single twenties and thirties having fun in promiscuous relationships. When she hit her early forties, she realized that her biological clock was ticking and her market value was declining. So, she decided to settle down. She was still attractive for her age and could probably have chosen from numerous sober and stable men who were no doubt pursuing her. But those men didn't have the social or financial status she wanted. So she solved her dilemma by getting herself knocked up by a multimillionaire whose personal history virtually screamed "Danger." He did the honorable thing and married her. She divorced him within a couple of years because of his alleged violence and alcoholism. Their unfortunate child grew into an adult with a buffet of psychological problems. But I never heard this woman take any responsibility for the calamities that befell her and her child as a result of her choice to wait until her forties to hook a rotten man because he was rich. It was all his fault.

In another case, I was interviewing an elderly widow who outlived three husbands. She was beautiful when she was young, but now was just another broken down old woman. In spite of that, she still managed to trowel on a thick layer of makeup and decorate herself like a Christmas tree each morning. She divorced her first husband when she was forty. Within two years she married a widower who was more than thirty years older than herself. She described him as the love of her life. I'm sure his being filthy rich and providing her with a lavish lifestyle had nothing to do with her affections. He died of natural causes about seven years later. Within a year she remarried another recent widower who was a financially-secure retired military officer. He was also was also a chain-smoking alcoholic. She made the rest of that man's life miserable by constantly badgering him about his smoking, his drinking, and his occasionally abrasive personality. During my interview of her, I finally tired of hearing her complain about her first and third husbands, so I said, "Well, you picked them." She replied "I didn't pick them. They picked me." I said "Maybe so. But you had a choice. You knew who they were when they proposed to you. You could have said no." She just looked down with an angry expression on her face and muttered unintelligibly. Each of those men had something that she thought she could exploit. In the end she got what her dissembling exploitation deserved.

In another case, a client in her sixties was going through a nasty divorce with her second husband of thirty years. During a phone interview she told me that her first husband was the love of her life, but that he was an alcoholic. Their marriage ended when he put a gun to his head and blew his brains out. She was telling me at length what a terrible person her current husband was. I finally interrupted her and said "If he is so bad, why did you marry him?" Without missing a beat, she said "My mother made me!" I started laughing and said "Your mother made you? You were thirty-five years old when you married him! You had a choice! You're responsible!" She hung up on me and I haven't heard from her since. I then understood why her first husband blew his brains out. The alcohol had probably become ineffective at deadening the sound of her stupidity.

This kind of refusal to accept responsibility and blaming others is pervasive among legions of modern young and not so young women today. They get jobs they can't do, take on responsibilities they can't handle, and marry bad boys they can't control. When the boss fires them, or they fail to meet their responsibilities, or the bad boys dump them, they portray themselves as victims of misogynist bosses, unfair demands, or sociopaths. Unfortunately there is no shortage of stupid men who believe those lies and come galloping to the rescue.

If you're a man who assumes women are victims and you are easily overcome by your natural instincts to rescue "damsels in distress," you need drive a stake through the heart those assumptions and instincts as quickly as possible. With rare exception, women are not victims and you should not treat them as such. Each year, countless men foolishly thrust themselves into the middle of angry disputes between men and women, knowing nothing about the relationship of the combatants or the reasons for the disputes. Some of those men end up injured or dead for their misguided meddling. Unless it is absolutely necessary to save a woman's life, mind your own business! A woman who can deliver a baby after nine months of pregnancy can survive an ass-kicking as well or better than you can. And you should consider the possibility that the ass-kicking was not totally undeserved. Let the police deal with it.

PSYCHOLOGICAL WARFARE

The theories concocted by psychologists about the complicated emotional and psychological dynamics of women who remain in abusive relationships are nonsense. The relationship is usually portrayed as one in which a controlling abusive man takes advantage of a fearful innocent woman. Women have been selling that fertilizer for decades, and men have been buying it by the truckload. The dynamics in those relationships are usually much more two dimensional than presented. Simply put, women want to control men. Men are physically stronger than women. So women must resort to psychological warfare to make a man angry. An angry man is an irrational man, and an irrational man can be controlled. The bigger and more athletic a man is, the more vulnerable he is to being manipulated into becoming angry. Why? Because big athletic guys are accustomed to controlling other people by the path of least resistance; intimidation. Since smaller men cave in to them to avoid being beaten up, intimidation becomes a default program for the big athletic guys to maintain control of others. So when those guys are suddenly confronted by an aggressively contentious and uncooperative woman who won't back down, they have no backup plan and go to step two in their default program; brute force.

Psychological warfare is a woman's weapon of choice for controlling a physically stronger male opponent. That's why many of the high profile domestic battery cases reported in the media are wealthy professional athletes and movie stars who beat up their antagonistic wives or girlfriends.

In most relationships where a woman complains about ongoing abuse, she is not the one being abused. She is the abuser. For her, pushing her physically stronger husband's buttons until he comes unglued to the point of smacking her is enormously satisfying and probably part of her long term strategy. She wins. He goes to jail and she gets the attention and sympathy that she craves. If he is rich and she divorces him, she wins again. She'll get her freedom and half of everything he has. Not a bad haul for a little pain and few bruises, both of which will disappear in few days. The following anecdotes from my law enforcement days and investigation files are good illustrations:

A young man spent six hours of his day-off doing home and yard maintenance in mid ninety degree weather. Hot and tired after finishing his work, he stretched out on a shaded lounge chair on his deck to rest and re-hydrate. His wife, who had spent her day in their air conditioned home, came outside and said "You need to go to the store and get me some Mountain Dew." Being hot, tired, and now a little annoyed by her bad timing and dictatorial tone, he replied "You know where the keys are. Drive yourself to the store." She reminded him that she was pregnant, and she again ordered him to "Go get me my Mountain Dew!" He reminded her that she was only two months pregnant, and that her pregnancy didn't stop her from partying with her girlfriends the previous evening. She continued to badger him until he couldn't stand it anymore. He got up and headed for the door to go into the house to get away from her. She stepped in front of him to block his path. Each time he tried to go around her, she side-stepped into his path and became more verbally belligerent. He anticipated her final attempt. He put his arm forward to prevent her from getting in front of him. She tried to push his arm out of the way. He stiffened it. Since he was bigger and stronger, she ended up pushing herself backwards off his arm. She did a faux fall over a lounge chair. She was uninjured, but she called 911. When the police arrived, she told them that her husband pushed her over the lounge chair and that she was pregnant. In spite of her husband's contradictory explanation of the event, the police arrested him and charged him with domestic battery on a pregnant female. That's a felony. On the advice of his attorney, and to avoid the possibility of a five year prison sentence if he went to trial and lost, he accepted a plea deal for probation. The probation deal included the permanent loss of his right to possess a firearm. The only recreation this young man had that he really looked forward to was a yearly hunting trip with a few of his buddies. The loss of his right to possess a firearm permanently ended that recreational outlet. They eventually divorced. But his firearms rights and hunting days were gone forever.

A client was separated from his wife and was going through nasty divorce. His efforts to reach a fair settlement with her had proven fruitless. Even his attorney was dumbfounded by how vicious and intransigent she had become. One day he had to meet with her in the parking lot of a college to discuss several issues. Their discussion quickly degenerated into her yelling and cursing at him. He kept his cool and told her that he wasn't going to stand there and be yelled at. When he turned and began walking away from her, she snatched his cellphone from his back pocket. He turned around and told her to return his phone. She refused, but she didn't try to run away with it. She stood there and taunted him by waving his cellphone in his face and continuing to insult him. He remembered that I had warned him about women doing things like that to try to bait men into striking them. He followed my advice by turning around and walking away. His parting comment to her was "Fine. I'll just get another cellphone and have the service to that one turned off." She began screaming as if she was being beaten. He turned around and saw her rolling on the pavement and yelling "You hit me! I'm calling the police!" Fortunately for him an employee of the college was preparing to leave for the day and witnessed the entire episode from his car in the parking lot. After the clients wife left the scene, the employee approached my client and told him that he witnessed the incident. The college security officer made a written report of the incident at my clients request and included a statement by the witness. The police couldn't arrest my client for battery or arrest his wife for filing a false report because of the conflicting statements.

In another case, a young woman got into an argument with her boyfriend at his house. She went outside, began slapping and punching herself, and ripped her blouse. She then called 911 and reported that her boyfriend had beaten her up. When the police arrived and saw physical evidence consistent with the woman's allegation, they arrested her boyfriend in spite of his denials. Fortunately for him, his girlfriend did not see the elderly man and woman who were watching her entire performance from their unlit front porch two houses down and across the street from the boyfriends house. The man and his wife walked over to the police and told them everything they saw. The boyfriend was released and the girlfriend was arrested for filing a false crime report.

The moral of these stories is simple. If you don't do what your wife wants you to do, she will try to destroy you. She'll lie to the police, beat herself up, steal your cellphone, screw your best friend, key your car, burn your clothes, smash your guitar, destroy your gaming console, or do anything else that she knows will cause you physical, emotional or financial pain. For modern women, inflicting pain on a man is better than sex.

A woman will try to use the power of the state to enforce her control over you. It is not uncommon for women to call the police to report abuse. But when the police show up and pull out the handcuffs to arrest her alleged abuser, the woman who complained will often yell "No! Don't arrest him!" When the police ask her what she wants them to do, the typical reply is something like "I just want you to make him stop." Her objective is to use the power of the government to force her husband to be her obedient slave. Since the police don't have the right or the power to do that, all they can do is arrest him. When they do arrest him, more often than not, the woman who made the complaint will show up at the state attorney's office the next day to withdraw it.

For the record, I do not like men or women who are abusive. I believe that we all, men and women, should be as kind and patient toward one another as circumstances allow. But I reject the modern social and cultural narrative that, for all practical purposes, defines domestic abuse as anything a man does that his wife does not approve of. Let's be clear. An unprovoked verbal threat is abuse. Unprovoked physical aggression is abuse. But knocking a belligerent egocentric argumentative harpy on her backside when she tries to stop you from getting away from her, or when she refuses your order to back off after angrily and aggressively invading your personal space, is not abuse. And any man who has a reasonable amount of experience dealing with modern women can tell you that being belligerent, egocentric, and argumentative are hallmarks of the modern woman's personality. The only variations are in degree of subtlety.

EQUALITY VS TYRANNY

"Call to mind all the regulations respecting women by which our ancestors curbed their licence and made them obedient to their husbands, and yet in spite of all those restrictions you can scarcely hold them in. If you allow them to pull away these restraints and wrench them out one after another, and finally put themselves on an equality with their husbands, do you imagine that you will be able to tolerate them? From the moment that they become your fellows they will become your masters." ~ Marcus Porcius Cato, 234 – 149 BC, aka Cato the Elder and the Wise. A Roman soldier, senator and historian. From The History of Rome, Vol. 5, by Titus Livius, translated by Rev. Canon Roberts.

Women don't want equality with men. They want total control; not only of personal relationships, but of everything else. The word for that is "tyranny." They have made enormous progress towards achieving that objective in recent years. And, as Cato implicitly observed, it is our fault as men for letting them get away with it.

If you are a man who has had the misfortune of having to work under a woman in a position of authority over you, you might have noticed her unnecessarily confrontational and autocratic management style. You might also have noticed her penchant for screwing things up and then not taking responsibility for it. A woman's natural algorithmic default programming for dealing with the problems she creates is:

1. Admit nothing.
2. Deny everything.
3. Demand proof.
4. Blame others.

Here is another anecdote from my law enforcement days:

About fifteen other law enforcement investigators and I were at a morning briefing to discuss three search warrants that were to be simultaneously executed later that day at three different locations. Since the warrants were related to environmental crimes, an equal number of non-sworn regulatory personnel with expertise in that arena were assigned to the operation. The person in charge of the operation was a belligerent middle-aged female law enforcement lieutenant. She announced that the regulatory personnel would go in first, followed by the law enforcement investigators. Upon hearing this, some of the regulatory personnel became visibly concerned. The execution of any search warrant is potentially dangerous, and the scene needs to be secured by armed sworn personnel before exposing non-sworn personnel to potential danger. My male supervisor, who was also a lieutenant, noticed the concern of the regulatory personnel. He politely interrupted the female lieutenant and explained to the regulatory personnel that the female lieutenant meant to say that the regulatory personnel would follow the law enforcement personnel in after the scene was secure. The regulatory personnel breathed a sigh of relief and the female lieutenant thanked my supervisor for explaining what she "meant to say." But she never got over him correcting her. Several months later she tried to get him fired. She suborned her unethical minions within the unit to lie about him. That resulted in an internal investigation and subsequent charges being made. He hired a lawyer and he fought back. Realizing their untenable position, the lack of supporting evidence, and the conflicting "witness statements", the agency dropped the charges and settled with him. The female lieutenant became a captain at another agency. I personally knew several investigators who worked with her at several other agencies. They described her an an incompetent idiot whose cases were messes that they constantly had to clean up. When they cleaned up her messes and polished her cases, she took the credit. I have to assume that she applied for the captain's position on her knees. She certainly didn't get it on her professional competence or personal ethics. She has since retired. But I suspect that she is still incompetent, unethical, and on her knees.

Women, such as the lieutenant, are everywhere in today's society. Using any means at their disposal, they aggressively seek positions of power that their intellects, experience, character, or physical abilities do not qualify them for. Those women are often hired or promoted over more qualified men because of gender quotas, or because they screwed the boss, or because the agency head was obsessed with appearing "politically correct." When those women perform below established standards, they are rarely held accountable. In private businesses they are promoted or transferred to positions where they can do less harm. If their conduct was criminal, they are given an opportunity to resign, but they are rarely prosecuted. If they are government employees or elected officials, they blame their substandard performance on their subordinates. If their transgressions were criminal acts that leave the government no respectable alternative but to prosecute them, they are given sweet plea deals, withheld adjudications, and a few meaningless hours of community service. Statistics don't lie. Women are routinely given breaks for transgressions that similarly offending men are fired or incarcerated for.

Women demand to be treated as equal to men, and they have the support of feminist legislators, jurists, university professors, social justice warriors, and movie stars. But they want accommodations or exemptions for their inability to perform at the same level as men.

If you ever hear one of those feminists boasting about her equality, ask her one of these simple questions: "If you called 911 at two o'clock in the morning because a muscular, six-foot five, two-hundred and fifty pound naked man with a butcher knife and a hard-on was trying to kick your door down, do you want a male or a female officer to show up to deal with him?" Or "If your house was on fire and you were confined to bed because your leg was broken, do you want a male or a female firefighter to show up to carry you to safety?" So much for "Equality." If you ever see a feminists being chased or beaten by an angry man, just smile and wave at her as you drive by.

IT'S ALL ABOUT ME

Dr. Paul Julius Möbius was a German neurologist who lived from 1853 to 1907. In his magnum opus, "Über den physiologischen Schwachsinn des Weibes" (On the physiological imbecility of women), he wrote: "Dazu kommt der Mangel an Sachlichkeit, der Wünsche zu Gründen und Abneigungen zu Beweisen macht." The English translation of that is "Then there is the lack of objectivity, which turns wishes into reasons and aversions into proof."

What Dr. Möbius was describing is a woman's well known propensity to view the world through the lens of her own subjective emotions and desires, rather than through the lens of objective reality and logic. The results of that propensity create havoc in the lives of almost everyone in her wake. Adult men have some degree of insulation from that havoc because they can walk away from her, even if they have to take some personal damage with them. But a child under a woman's care and custody does not have that luxury. Helpless children die each year inside sweltering motor vehicles because mommy forgot they were in a safety seat just a few feet behind her when she parked the vehicle and got out. Some die in swimming pools or other bodies of water because mommy wasn't paying attention. Still others die from gobbling down medicine from a container that mommy carelessly left the childproof top off of. Was she distracted by concerns of a possible terrorist attack or a life threatening medical diagnosis? No. It's more likely that she was agonizing over the new gray hairs and wrinkles she saw in the mirror that morning. Or the five pounds of weight she gained that week. Or a secret adulterous rendezvous she was planning. Or how she was going to pay for those sexy pumps she saw at the mall. Yes, when push comes to shove, to one degree or another, a woman will put her own selfish carnal and material desires ahead of every other living creature or moral consideration.

Many young women today say they want a husband and children, but not necessarily in that order. Instead they put off marriage because they're having too much fun partying with bad-boys. When they hit their mid thirties or forties, look in the mirror and see the wrinkles and sags, they start looking for a rich handsome man to marry them and give them children. By that time the rich handsome men are already married or are dating younger and better looking women. And the odds of her giving birth to a child with a birth defect is significantly increased. The incidents of a thirty or forty year-old woman giving birth to a child with downs syndrome is 1 in 900 and 1 in 100 respectively, as opposed to 1 in 2000 for a twenty year-old. But women don't care. They want what they want, and the welfare of anyone and everyone else be damned.

In 2018, a woman in Indiana was sentenced to 120 years in prison for stabbing to death her seven year-old son and three year-old daughter. Why? Because her husband had filed for divorce and she did not want him to have custody of the them. If you think that is an unusual case, you're wrong. There have been many similar incidents in the past few decades, and the problem is getting worse. Besides that, there is no significant difference between a woman who murders her own children to stop her soon-to-be ex-husband from having custody of them, and the tens of thousands of women each year who pay doctors to assassinate their unborn children because they don't want stretch marks, or the inconvenience of raising a child, or the stigma that justly goes along with being a slut.

THE FAMOUS AND THE INFAMOUS

Florence Nightingale, 1820 – 1910, was a truly great lady. As a British nurse, social reformer and statistician, she is best known as the founder of modern nursing. She became known as "The Lady with the Lamp" because of her sacrificial night-time nursing rounds to tend to wounded soldiers during the Crimean War. Nightingale trained nurses and worked closely with other women, so she was well acquainted with their character. What did nurse Nightingale have to say about them? "Women have no sympathy, and my experience of women is almost as large as Europe."

On the opposite side of that coin is Lucrezia Marinella, 1571 – 1653. Marinella was an Italian poet, author, and an advocate of women's rights. She was also an early prototype of the modern American woman as illustrated in the following quote: "It is an amazing thing to see in our city the wife of a shoemaker, or a butcher, or a porter dressed in silk with chains of gold at the throat, with pearls and rings of good value. . . and then to see her husband cutting the meat, all smeared with cow's blood, poorly dressed. . . but whoever considers this carefully will find it reasonable, because it is necessary that the lady, even if low born and humble, be draped with such clothes for her natural excellence and dignity, and the man be less adorned as if a slave, or a little ass, born to her service." That last line is precisely how modern American women view men; ". . . as if a slave, or a little ass, born to her service."

Here is another quote from a more recent and arguably less virtuous woman: "May your wife and children get raped, right in the ass." That was Aileen Wuornos' parting comment to the jurors who convicted her of multiple counts of murder. Aileen Wuornos, 1956 – 2002, was a convicted serial killer and prostitute who murdered seven men in Florida during 1989 and 1990 by shooting them at point blank range. She was executed by lethal injection in 2002.

I don't view Wuornos as a monstrous anomaly. I see her as a refreshingly honest woman. Some would argue that Aileen's dysfunctional childhood was the root cause of her murderously antisocial behavior. I would argue that it was just a coincidental parallel. I've seen too many other cases of adult women who had good childhoods, yet still became prostitutes, drug addicts, robbers, thieves, child abusers, and murderers; and then rationalized that someone or something other than their own native depravity was to blame for their behavior.

And there are plenty of practicing psychologists and psychiatrists who will validate their excuses. Here's another endearing quote from Wuornos: "I robbed them, and I killed them as cold as ice, and I would do it again, and I know I would kill another person because I've hated humans for a long time."

I have interacted with enough women during my lifetime to tell you that the dark malevolence expressed by Wuornos bubbles just beneath the surface in most of them. It might not manifest itself at quite the same level of brutality, but it's there nonetheless. And the current social and cultural climate allows that malevolence to ooze from their pores like toxic waste from a decaying storage drum.

WHAT ABOUT TRUST?

"Trust not a woman when she weeps, for it is her nature to weep when she wants her will." - Socrates, 470 – 399 BC. Greek philosopher and foundational figure in western philosophy.

You should never trust a woman, but especially when she cries. For most men, a woman's tears are like kryptonite is for Superman. It causes him to become weak and confused. Unless you are a man who has disciplined yourself to have no emotional response to a woman's tears, you should run from her at the first quiver of her lip or the slightest glazing of her eyes.

Women use crying as a form of emotional manipulation. Am I saying that a woman's tears are fake? No. I'm saying that women cry real tears because they are genuinely unhappy about not getting what they want or about being held accountable for their bad behavior. That's what spoiled brats do. One would hope that an adult woman would be able to handle adult disappointments and responsibilities without crying like a six year-old. But most of them can't. They suffer from what my dear departed daddy called "acute infantilism." And that is a condition they have no intention of outgrowing.

Why should they? It's been working for them for thousands of years.

Of the scores of shoplifters I arrested during my career, about eighty percent of them were women. Most of the men I arrested for shoplifting went to jail without crying or making excuses. Nearly all of the women I arrested for shoplifting cried like spoiled brats, made ridiculous excuses for their crime, and begged me to let them go. When tears didn't work, some of those women offered me sexual favors. When I didn't take them up on that offer, they became as vicious as rabid animals. As seventeenth century English playwright and poet William Congreve noted in his drama The Mourning Bride, "Heav'n has no Rage, like Love to Hatred turn'd, Nor Hell a Fury, like a Woman scorn'd."

Here is an interesting side note about shoplifters: Most men shoplifters steal beer, cigarettes, or food. Most women shoplifters steal cosmetics, perfume, jewelry, or fashion accessories. Do you see the difference? Men steal to satisfy a physical craving. Women steal to satisfy a psychological craving for attention. Reaching into a man's head to help him control his physical craving is doable. Reaching into a woman's head to help her control her psychological craving for attention is nearly impossible because she is psychologically inaccessible. She has built a virtually impenetrable psychological fortress as a defense mechanisms. The foundation of that fortress is denial. A problem must be recognized before it can be fixed. And women are notorious for denying that there is anything wrong with them.

LIAR LIAR

Nineteenth century German philosopher Arthur Schopenhauer, 1788 – 1860, wrote what I consider to be the definitive essay explaining female behavior as it relates to honesty. Following is an excerpt from that essay. The translation is by Mrs. Rudolf Dircks:

"For as lions are furnished with claws and teeth, elephants with tusks, boars with fangs, bulls with horns, and the cuttlefish with its dark, inky fluid, so Nature has provided woman for her protection and defence with the faculty of dissimulation, and all the power which Nature has given to man in the form of bodily strength and reason has been conferred on woman in this form. Hence, dissimulation is innate in woman and almost as characteristic of the very stupid as of the clever. Accordingly, it is as natural for women to dissemble at every opportunity as it is for those animals to turn to their weapons when they are attacked; and they feel in doing so that in a certain measure they are only making use of their rights. Therefore a woman who is perfectly truthful and does not dissemble is perhaps an impossibility. This is why they see through dissimulation in others so easily; therefore it is not advisable to attempt it with them. From the fundamental defect that has been stated, and all that it involves, spring falseness, faithlessness, treachery, ungratefulness, and so on. In a court of justice women are more often found guilty of perjury than men. It is indeed to be generally questioned whether they should be allowed to take an oath at all."

One of the most obvious manifestations of a woman's dissimulation is in her appearance. Makeup, lipstick, mascara, false eyelashes, hair dye, wigs, push-up bras, face lifts, butt lifts, Botox injections, etc. are all designed with one purpose in mind; to deceive other people into thinking that she is something that she is not. And what is she not? Pretty and sexy. Those attributes must be artificially created and are therefore counterfeit. The truth is that about eighty percent of any woman's beauty can be erased in less than a minute by stripping her naked and wiping off her makeup. When you consider the massive amounts of print and television advertising directed at selling the previously described goods and services to women, and the massive amounts of time and money that women spend on those goods and services, it should be obvious that a woman's appearance is more than just a casual concern to her. It's a psychotic obsession. And it is not a new one.

In his "Jenseits von Gut und Böse" (Beyond Good and Evil), German philosopher Friedrich Nietzsche, 1844 – 1900, was clearly aware of that obsession when he wrote "Nichts ist von Anbeginn an dem Weibe fremder, widriger, feindlicher als Wahrheit, - seine grosse Kunst ist die Lüge, seine höchste Angelegenheit ist der Schein und die Schönheit." In her translation of Nietzsche's work, Helen Zimmern translated that passage as: "From the very first, nothing is more foreign, more repugnant, or more hostile to woman than truth—her great art is falsehood, her chief concern is appearance and beauty."

1800 years before Friedch Nietzsche, the Roman poet Juvenal, (Decimus Junius Juvenalis), c. 55 AD – c. second century AD, wrote what is translated as:

"There is nothing that a woman will not permit herself to do. Nothing that she deems shameful. And when she encircles her neck with green emeralds and fastens huge pearls to her elongated ears, so important is the business of beautification; so numerous are the tiers and stories piled one another on her head that she pays no attention to her own husband."

The deception in a modern woman's appearance is compounded by the lies she tells to try to justify the deception. "I don't care what men think. I just want to look nice for me", or "I'm wearing just a little makeup", or "I have to dress like this to look professional at the office", or "I don't have anything else to wear", or "It was on sale" or "This is my natural hair color", etc. The lies are nearly infinite.

If a man, wearing a ski mask and carrying a shotgun, walked into a bank, the women in that bank would assume that he was there to rob it. If one of those same women dressed herself in a push-up bra, a low cut sweater, a short tight skirt, spiked heels and enough makeup to be a kabuki dancer, and then walked into a sports bar full of men, and any man there suggested that she was there to rob some witless idiot by getting him to buy her a drink or a meal, every woman within earshot would lose her mind. A woman who behaves as the one described in the sports bar scenario is trying to gain access to a man's wallet by causing his sexual impulses to short circuit his judgment. In some cases she might just be looking for a one-time free meal or drink. In other cases she might be looking for an extended relationship in which one particular man will regularly buy her dinner, jewelry or whatever else she wants, in exchange for sex. And if other men label her a whore, women will become outraged. But outrage does not nullify truth. By definition a whore is someone who engages in sexual activity in exchange for payment. The particular type of sexual activity or the form of payment is irrelevant. And monogamy or marriage license does not transform a whore into a virtuous woman. A woman who marries a man for his money or for the material goodies he can provide for her, regardless of how kind or considerate she is toward him, is not a wife. She's a high priced hooker with a long term lease.

Philo Judaeus, c 20 BC – c 50 AD, better known as Philo of Alexandria, was a Hellenistic Jewish philosopher who lived in Alexandria in the Roman province of Egypt. In "The Works of Philo, volume I", translated by Charles Duke Yongel, Philo describes the general appearance of a whore as follows:

". . . luxuriously dressed in the guise of a harlot and prostitute, with mincing steps, rolling her eyes about with excessive licentiousness and desire, by which baits she entraps the souls of the young, looking about with a mixture of boldness and impudence, holding up her head, and raising herself above her natural height, fawning and giggling, having the hair of her head dressed with most superfluous elaborateness, having her eyes pencilled, her eyebrows covered over, using incessant warm baths, painted with a fictitious colour, exquisitely dressed with costly garments, richly embroidered, adorned with armlets, and bracelets, and necklaces, and all other ornaments which can be made of gold, and precious stones, and all kinds of female decorations; loosely girdled, breathing of most fragrant perfumes, thinking the whole market her home; a marvel to be seen in the public roads, out of the scarcity of any genuine beauty, pursuing a bastard elegance."

It almost sounds like Philo was describing the herd of irksome actresses who stampede the red carpet each year at the Academy Awards.

Mistake me not! I am not an advocate for prostitution or for hiring prostitutes! But given the choice between a prostitute whose services you can unilaterally and immediately terminate without consequences if she becomes a fat contentious virago; or a woman who becomes a fat contentious virago, and can then make your life miserable for decades to come because you foolishly signed a legally binding long term contract with her, which do you think makes more sense?

There is actually a third option that too

many men fail to seriously consider. Avoid romantic entanglements with women to begin with. In most instances it is better to be alone. You won't die or go crazy if you don't have a woman to share your life with. Make platonic friendships with like-minded men. The list of profitable, productive and emotionally satisfying things that men can accomplish together is almost endless. Focus on your own physical, mental, emotional, and spiritual health. What will women do without you? Who cares? Let them devour the low hanging fruit; (i.e. imbecilic men who think with their peckers, and who have no self-respect, no self-control, and no worthwhile ambition.) What will you do without women? Achieve great things!

"I Don't Have Time For Both A Wife And An Airplane." - Wilbur Wright, Brother of Orville Wright. Both life long bachelors and American aviation pioneers credited with inventing, building, and flying the world's first successful motor-operated airplane.

Here are a few other ways women routinely lie. Teenage women who are not old enough to attend adult venues will lie about their age to gain access to those venues. I lost track of the number of times I was called to bars to remove under-aged women who had either no ID or who used fraudulent or altered ID to get in. Those women were wearing heavy makeup and whorish attire. It was usually the owner who called because those women were hitting on the legal male customers and the owner didn't want to lose his liquor license if he didn't report the underage women and the police discovered them inside his establishment. Why do these young women do this? Bragging rights, blackmail, prostitution, or just unbridled concupiscence.

Older single / divorced women (aka "cougars"), who are rapidly running out of options, lie about their age to try to deceive men with money into considering them for marriage or long term relationships. There is very little that a single or divorced cougar will not do to hook such a man. That includes getting herself knocked up by him before he can figure out what she is up to. Even if he won't marry her, she'll get the next best thing; eighteen years of child support payments. And in case you don't know, attorneys and judges base those payment's on the father's income, not on the actual needs of the child. The wealthier the man is, the more money mommy can get for child support. Everything over and above the minimum that she has to spend for the child's survival will go to satisfy her own carnal and material appetites. She'll buy designer clothes and gourmet meals for herself at expensive boutiques and fancy restaurants. But she'll buy the child's clothes and food at thrift stores and fast-food drive-thrus.

One method women use to get knocked up when the man won't cooperate with her plan is "sperm-jacking." Sperm-jacking is the practice of surreptitiously collecting a man's sperm for the purposes of inseminating herself without the man's knowledge or consent. Here are a few sperm-jacking methods to beware of.

- Secretly poking a pinhole through the center of a sealed condom wrapper to damage the tip of the condom so it will leak or burst when the man ejaculates.
- Secretly recovering a man's spent condom from a trashcan to inseminate herself with its contents.
- Performing fellatio on a man and allowing him to ejaculate in her mouth. Then surreptitiously spiting the semen into a suitable device, perhaps even her own hand, and forcing the semen into her own vagina. (No, I'm not making that up.)

As an alternative to sperm-jacking, a woman who is on birth control might stop taking her birth control without telling her partner. Even married women cannot be trusted. Married women who made agreements with their husbands concerning the number of children they would have together have been known to change their minds. If such a woman tells her husband that she wants another child, and he refuses to cooperate, she will resort to any of the previously described methods to get pregnant. A woman considers having a child a divine right that justifies her deceit. And she thinks her husband has a divine obligation to carry the resulting burden of her unilateral decision in spite of her deception and her breach of their agreement.

There are pregnant women and online vendors who sell positive pregnancy tests. Who do you think buys those tests? Women. Why would a woman who is not pregnant buy a positive pregnancy test? To show it to her boyfriend to try to pressure him into marrying her, or to extort money from him for a fictitious abortion.

Suppose a woman has sex with ten different men during a short time frame. (and that is not a particularly high number for women today). And suppose she then successfully hits each of them up for $500 for an abortion. That's five thousand dollars of tax free income that she could use to pay her rent and utilities for six months if some idiot man is not already paying them for her.

If any woman ever tries to pressure you into marrying her or giving her money by showing you a positive pregnancy test, ask her to take another test while you watch and wait for the results to develop. If she refuses, dump her on the spot. If she agrees and the test is negative, learn your lesson and terminate the relationship. If it comes back positive and you have good reasons to doubt that the child is yours, tell her that you want a prenatal DNA test. If she refuses, abandon her and don't pay any of her bills. If she gets an abortion, let it be completely on her head. If she carries and delivers the child, and then sues you for child support, the courts will order a paternity test before making you pay if you contest paternity.

Some older women lie about their age simply because they are terrified of growing old alone and having so little income that they have to choose between buying food or buying makeup and jewelry. Tough choice. They will become angry, lie, or refuse to answer if a man asks them how old they are. Some of those women are so delusional that they actually believe the modern name-it-and-claim-it heresy that physical realities can be created ex nihilo by positive affirmation. If a fifty-pound overweight forty-year-old woman repeatedly tells herself that she is really a fit and trim thirty year-old who can hook a handsome and wealthy husband to take care of her, and that she can carry and deliver a healthy child, she will eventually believe it. And no objectively rational force on earth will convince her otherwise.

THE MARRIAGE COUNSELING SCAM

When married couples are having problems and go for counseling, a chief complaint by the wife is often a lack of communication from her husband. Her complaint is probably valid. But the reason for his lack of communication is rarely explored beyond a superficial assumption or accusation that he is just an insensitive jerk. Obviously his lack of communication was not always a problem. Before they married, he must have communicated with her enough for her to go on dates with him and accept his marriage proposal. And her acceptance of his proposal suggests that she liked him enough to marry him. What happened?

A husband stops communicating with his wife when he realizes the futility of it. It is an emotionally and physically exhausting exercise that produces no fruit at all or fruit that is so bitter that he is incapable of consuming it without vomiting. A wife wants communication from her husband, not because she actually cares what he thinks or how he feels. She want's communication from him because:

1. It validates her existence by giving her the attention that she constantly craves.
2. It provides her with information about his

likes and dislikes; information she will weaponize against him to make his life miserable, either at home or in court.

Men are results oriented creatures. If repeated efforts at a task produce no measurable positive results, they abandon the effort and move on to something else. That applies to communication with women. And since women are notorious for either ignoring or intentionally doing the opposite of what their husbands ask them to do or not do, there is little point in talking to them. This is demonstrated by a wife's consistent refusal to comply with the simplest requests her husband makes. Things like putting the top back on the toothpaste tube, replacing the toilet paper when it runs out, turning off lights when not needed, locking the car and house doors at night before going to bed, or filling the car's gas tank before the low fuel light comes on. Is her refusal to comply with such simple requests that big of a deal? You bet it is! Why? Because it is a passive-aggressive non-verbal manifestation of her contempt for him that will eventually manifest itself in infidelity, violence, or divorce.

When a woman communicates with men generally, and with her husband in particular, that communication usually takes the form of virtue signaling, obfuscation, lying, shit-testing, or passive-aggression intended to make him mad or manipulate him into doing what she wants him to do. This kind of communication is destructive to any healthy human relationship, regardless of gender. A man would not maintain a platonic friendship with another man who behaved that way. Why a woman thinks he should tolerate it from her simply because she has a vagina and a heartbeat is a mystery.

Marriage counselors claim that they want to foster strong and healthy marital relationships. Whatever these counselors may know about matters related to anything else, they obviously know very little about female nature within a marital context. I recently saw the following quote by a man identified as Sam Isaacs. Sam has clearly figured it out:

"On the 7th week of marriage counseling I turned to both the counselor and my wife (now ex) and I said 'I've just realized we have spent the last 7 weeks talking about me and everything I'm doing wrong. What did you do wrong? What is your responsibility here?' Both of them looked shocked and didn't know how to answer. I believe I hit the nail on the head for the whole western world."

Modern marriage counseling is crafted to

accommodate the selfish and unrealistic expectations of women. I've talked to many married men who went to marital counseling with their wives. As with Mr. Isaacs, those men described counseling sessions which focused almost entirely on what they did or didn't do that made their wives unhappy. The counselors in those cases showed little interest in what the wife did or didn't do that made the husbands unhappy. Most of those men were eventually divorced by their wives for failing to meet unreasonable expectations. Those who didn't end up divorced remained married and miserable. A few of them became so despondent that they finally gave up and took their own lives.

I am not defending "bad behavior" by husbands toward their wives. I just don't accept the modern presumption that a woman is entitled to unilaterally decide what bad behavior is, and that she is the sole arbiter and final authority on the subject. So let me tell you what "bad behavior" is. Bad behaviors are drunkenness and adultery; unprovoked cursing, yelling, striking or threatening; or not providing for the basic physical and material needs that one is ethically obligated to provide. But refusing to passively tolerate your wife disrespectfully treating you like her personal slave or like a disobedient child is not bad behavior.

I have heard psychologists explicitly promote the absurd narrative that women are gentle, patient, kind, and carnally temperate by nature. I've also heard some of those same psychologists implicitly promote the equally absurd counter-narrative that men are ignorant insensitive brutes who would die without the care and guidance of their wives. Neither of those narratives have anything to do with objective reality. And the psychologists who promote those narratives are either moronic or demonic.

If a woman does behave in a way that psychologists can't avoid acknowledging as bad, many psychologists will go out of their way to make excuses for the behavior by blaming it on some undocumented childhood trauma or on some vague subjective "emotional abuse" the woman claims her husband chronically inflicts upon her. I sometimes wonder how many married men have sat silently gritting their teeth while some sanctimonious psychologist or counselor regurgitated clichés like:
- "You need to spend more time with her."
- "You need to tell her you love her more often."

- "You need to tell her how beautiful she is."
- "You need to be more romantic."
- "You need to be more sensitive to her emotional needs."
- "You need to. . ." blah blah blah ad nauseam.

And if the husband tries to explain that, while he was working his backside off to try to meet his wife's selfish expectations, she turned into a fat, lazy, contentious harridan who shows no interest in pleasing him, the counselor will either refuse to accept the husband's assessment as accurate, or will automatically assume that the wife's metamorphosis was caused by some undiagnosed hormonal imbalance. "Hormonal imbalance" is the default explanation for nearly all bad behaviors women display, because the possibility that she might just be a rotten human being at her core is taken off the table before the conversation even begins. I've heard some counselors suggest that nearly every kind of wickedness wives commit is due to some failure by her husband.

Marital counselors have been telling these lies to husbands and wives for so long that many husbands and wives actually believe them. When those marriages eventually implode, as nearly all of them do, many divorced husbands spend years feeling guilty for faults or failures that they don't really own. Meanwhile, the wives absolve themselves of genuine culpability because the counselors convinced them that their husbands were to blame for not meeting her "emotional needs." Maybe that's why it isn't unusual to hear about married women having adulterous relationships with male or lesbian counselors. I've come to the conclusion that most marriage counselors are just predators who exploit female gullibility and licentiousness for financial gain or sexual favors.

BEFORE AND AFTER

A single man's home is his well organized spartan castle. Kitchen drawers contain kitchen utensils. Kitchen cabinets contain cookware, dishes and food. One wall closet and one dresser are enough for all of his clothes and shoes. His medicine cabinet and under sink storage areas easily hold all of his hygiene and grooming needs. His car is a clean and mechanically well maintained machine. He is on time for appointments. And the occasional disagreements he has with other people are usually resolved peacefully.

When a man gets married, his wife becomes a princess, his castle becomes her palace, and he becomes her serf. If he is lucky, she will grant him a small space in the stable (garage) for a few of his things in exchange for his servile allegiance to her. She will replace his furniture and appliances; repaint his walls in colors akin to fresh vomit; fill his bookshelves with useless knickknacks and figurines; cram his closets with shoes, handbags and clothes, many of which still have price tags on them; cover his tables with magazines full of celebrity gossip and advertisements for cosmetics and clothes; fill his under-sink storage areas with her grooming products in half empty bottles that have either loose lids, no lids, or lids that have been carelessly (or perhaps intentionally) cross threaded so she can blame him when the bottles tip over and the contents leak out; She will fill his medicine cabinets with her prescription and non-prescription medications, many of which have expiration dates that have long since passed. She will appropriate his clean and mechanically well maintained car and turn it into a rolling pig pen whose tires are ten or more pounds low in pressure, whose crankcase is two or more quarts low on oil, and whose interior is a breeding ground for ants and roaches. If she presses him into service to drive her to an appointment, she will be late because she is never ready on time, but she will blame him for her tardiness. And if he has a minor dispute with another person in her presence, she will exacerbate the situation until he is incarcerated, hospitalized, or dead.

Anyone who tells you that you can have any significant lasting influence over a woman's thought processes or behavior by going to counseling or communicating with her is an idiot or a liar.

No matter what a woman tells you to the contrary, or how superficially nice she is to you, she does not see you as a human being worthy of her respect and cooperation. She sees you as an ATM, a vending machine, a mule, a bodyguard, a handyman, a landscaper, a chef, a chauffeur, a butler, a bellhop, a sex toy, a sperm donor, a door mat, or a disposal site for her toxic emotional waste. Any affection she offers you in return is counterfeit and limited to the bare minimum of what she thinks you will accept in exchange for providing her with one or more of those utilitarian services. If you stop providing them at the level she expects, she will find a replacement for you. And if anyone asks her why she terminated your services, she will tell them any lie that makes you look like a monster and makes her look like a victim instead of the selfish and uncooperative parasite that she really is.

NOTHING NEW UNDER THE SUN
Ecclesiastes 1:9 NIV

"There was a man in the land of Uz, whose name was Job; and that man was perfect and upright, and one that feared God, and eschewed evil. . . . His substance also was seven thousand sheep, and three thousand camels, and five hundred yoke of oxen, and five hundred she asses, and a very great household; so that this man was the greatest of all the men of the east."
~ Job 1:1 and 3, KJV.

Chapter 1 of Job doesn't tell us what Job looked like. But everything else about him was what most women say they dream of in a husband; a man who has high social status, is morally upright, and (cherry on top) is filthy rich. So, in chapter 2, when a grief stricken Job found himself sitting in an ash heap, using a piece of broken pottery to scrape the excruciating boils that covered his body after losing everything but his life, did his wife say "I love you" or "I'm here for you" or "We'll get though this together"? No. In more than forty chapters of this heroic Godly man's staggering physical and emotional suffering, the only thing she offered him was one piece of sarcastic advice which, if he had followed it, would have resulted in his eternal damnation. "Do you still hold fast your integrity? Curse God and die!" - Job 2:9 NASB.

If any woman that you have any kind of relationship with ever hurls sarcasm at you, no matter how subtle, even just once, you should immediately and permanently terminate that relationship. She just showed you her cards and what you can expect from her in the future. And yes, that includes your own mother. And when a woman gives you advice of any kind, you should analyze that advice carefully before following it. It probably contains some hidden agenda that will somehow benefit her at your expense. Besides that, to one degree or another, the lives of most women are train wrecks and their best advice is highly questionable. Whether the advice has to do with personal or professional relationships, physical or mental health, raising children or managing finances, her cars went off the rails at the top of a trestle and are on fire at the bottom of a ravine. Women who are obese, bi-polar, financially broke or have criminal children, will not hesitate to give other people advice on dieting, finding happiness, making money, or raising children. These women don't actually care about the well-being of the person they're giving advice to. They give advice because it makes them feel important and useful in the face of their realization that they are insignificant and useless. Her advice might be a little more subtle than "Curse God and die", but following it will probably be just as damning in the long run.

WHAT'S LOVE GO TO DO WITH IT?
"Love is the delusion that one woman differs from another." - H. L. Menkin, 1880 – 1956, American journalist, essayist, satirist, cultural critic, and scholar of American English.

When a woman tells you that she loves you, she is either lying or her definition of love is different than yours. And yes, again, that includes your mother. No woman will ever love you as much as she loves herself, and she won't love you in the same way you understand the word "love." For a woman, love describes the dopamine rush she gets from saying the words "I love you." It's a form of self-aggrandizing virtue signaling to try to convince you that she is a kind and loving person. Women say "I love you" with the same emotional depth and conviction that they have when they say "Ranch" to a waiter or waitress who asks them what kind of dressing they want on their salad.

And if a woman says to you "All I want is your love." she's lying again. What she means by "your love" is your willingness to surrender to her demands, validate her fantasies, and give her all of the material goodies her carnal heart desires. If or when you won't surrender to her demands, validate her fantasies, or give her those goodies, she will find some idiot who will in exchange for sex. There are plenty of them out there. And she will convince herself that her infidelity is justified by your failure to meet her expectations.

DUH!!!
"It has long been my belief that the sight of a good-looking woman lowers a man's IQ by at least twenty points. A man who doesn't happen to have twenty points he can spare can be in big trouble." - Dr. Thomas Sowell, 1930 – present. American economist, social theorist, and senior fellow at Stanford University's Hoover Institution.

A typical man today (i.e. - a man who is not tall, not handsome, not wealthy, not very smart, and not very experienced with women), is so mesmerized by even a semi-attractive woman who shows him a little attention and a little cleavage, he won't even wonder what she looks like beneath the quarter inch thick layer of makeup she is wearing, or what monstrous skeletons she is hiding in some rented warehouse because she couldn't fit all of them in her walk-in closets. Skeletons like: Multiple divorces, serial adultery, multiple abortions, sexually transmitted diseases, drug addiction, alcoholism, clinically diagnosed personality disorders, psychiatric institutionalization, psychotropic medications, previous incarcerations, active arrest warrants, evictions, outstanding civil judgments, bankruptcies, bad credit, unpaid debt, drug addicted criminal children, etc. If she gives that man just a little kindness and a little sex, both of which he is woefully unaccustomed to, he will propose marriage if for no other reason than he thinks it will save him from returning to the dreaded loneliness he lived in before she came into his life. A loneliness, by the way, that he will yearn for within a few short years of being legally shackled to her.

WHAT ABOUT HONOR?

"Honor is a male abstraction. Don't expect women to understand it." - author unknown

The proposition that an expensive diamond, an elaborate wedding and solemn vows before God will cause a woman to truly love you, cooperate with you, or stop her from seeking out illicit relationships with other men or women is a lie promoted by jewelry stores, florists, greeting card manufacturers, religious hucksters and a host of other people and corporations who stand to financially profit from you believing that lie.

A woman marries a man for what she can get out of him materially. The thought of bringing something of real value into the relationship rarely enters her mind. And if it does enter her mind, it will be based on what she thinks a man should want, rather than what he actually does want. If another man offers her something that is of greater value to her than what she is getting from her husband, she will take it. If her husband happens to have other things of value that she doesn't want to give up, she'll try to keep the other man and keep her husband from finding out about him. The other man will probably realize he is a side guy and won't care. He's enjoying the benefits of marriage without the aggravations and responsibilities. If the woman in question becomes pregnant from the other man, she will either have an abortion or commit paternity fraud.

Paternity fraud is when a woman tells her husband (or allows him to believe) that a child she is pregnant with or that she gave birth to is his when she knows it is not. Fortunately for men, modern DNA testing to determine paternity has stripped women of the ability to commit paternity fraud with impunity. Because paternity testing is a relatively recent development, many husbands have only recently discovered that children who they believed were theirs are actually the offspring of other men. Some men made that heart-breaking discovery after showering decades of love and hundreds of thousands of dollars on the child for things like food, shelter, clothes, medical and dental care, cars, insurance, college, weddings, etc. That may be why many court jurisdictions now require paternity testing before ordering a man to pay child support. The fact that courts, which have traditionally been grossly biased in favor of women, are waking up to this reality supports my point. If a pregnant woman thinks her husband might become suspicious and discover her infidelity through a paternity test if the child is born, she might murder her own unborn child rather than risk the embarrassment of being discovered as the lying cheating slut that she actually is. Most women are so concerned about their own pleasures and reputations, they would rather spend eternity in hell than remain faithful or confess their infidelity.

If you feel that you must marry, you best beware of the very real possibility that you could become a victim of paternity fraud. If you do, the emotional and financial consequences could be devastating and life long. You could end up devoting your life, your love, and your resources to another man's child while your unfaithful mate lies to you and to everyone else to hide her shame and maintain the illusion of respectability. In the meantime, she will continue to exploit you for the security that your love and financial support give her while she continues her infidelity, either in reality or in thought.

Another unpleasant possibility is that she will infect you with a sexually transmitted disease she acquires from another man. A man who is secretly having sex with your wife is probably having sex with other women (or perhaps men) as well, thereby greatly increasing the possibility of her becoming infected and passing that infection to you. If she discovers that she is infected, she will get the medical treatment she needs, but she will say nothing to you about it. When you develop symptoms and are diagnosed with the disease, you will naturally accuse her of cheating. But since she has already been treated and has no symptoms, she will turn the tables and accuse you. In a culture that mindlessly believes women over men, whose reputation do you think will be ruined?

If you still think that marriage or cohabiting is worth the risk, at least have the good sense to have a knowledgeable family law attorney draw up a prenuptial or domestic union contract that will hamper your future ex-wife's ability to rob you blind in court. Here are couple of anecdotes from my P.I. files:

A fifty year-old male client suspected that his forty year-old wife of ten years was cheating on him. This guy was smart, had a good job, a good reputation, and good opportunities for future advancement. During my investigation I discovered that his wife was having an ongoing sexual relationship with a muscular convicted felon who had an extensive criminal history. The client wasn't happy about it, but he handled it like a champ. Prior to marrying her, he had the good sense to have an attorney draw up a prenuptial agreement which she willingly signed. When their divorce was final, he walked away with his job, his pension, his paycheck, his wealth, his sanity and his dignity intact.

Another client was married for more than forty years. His adult children thought it would be fun to discover their ancestry through DNA testing. The DNA tests showed that one of his three adult children was really the child of one of his wife's former coworkers that she had sex with several decades earlier. His wife knew the truth all along. If not for the DNA test, he never would have known and she never would have confessed.

A woman who gleefully accepts your marriage proposal will lose her mind if you ask her to sign a prenuptial agreement. She will cry like a three-year-old and will try to shame you into abandoning the prenup. She will say something like "Waaaah!! If you really loved me, you wouldn't ask for a prenup!! Waaaah!!" And she will have the support of her friends and her family. If the two of you have any religious affiliation, she will also have the support of your pastor or priest. Do Not, under any circumstance, let anyone pressure you into abandoning the prenup!

Here's a secondary warning. If a woman wants to marry you badly enough to sign a prenup, be very afraid. Unless she is independently wealthy, emotionally stable and truly loves you, she has something else in the back of her mind or up her sleeve. She has either taken the prenup to her own attorney who found a loophole in it, or she is planning your untimely death after taking out a large life insurance policy in your name with herself as the beneficiary. And she won't have to poison you, push you down a flight of stairs, tamper with your brakes or hire a hit man to collect on that policy. All she will have to do is be herself. That means chronically whine, complain, nag, badger, gaslight, interrupt, criticize, and contradict you in the hundred different ways in which women are so highly skilled. Eventually your blood pressure will spike and you'll have a massive stroke or heart attack. If by some chance you don't die as a result, and are too physically disabled to end your own suffering, all you will be able to do is sit in your own waste and make unintelligible grunts while your wife's girlfriends gather around, pat you on the head, and tell her how wonderful she is for taking such good care of you. The plus side of that indignity is that it will probably cause you to have another stroke or heart attack that will turn your lights out permanently.

SAVE THE PLANET!
"These animals are very strange. One sometimes thinks they must be incapable of doing much harm, because they are incapable of doing any good. But I protest on my conscience that there is nothing so well able to ruin a state as they are." - Cardinal Armand Jean du Plessis, Duke of Richelieu, 1585 – 1642, French diplomatist and statesman writing about women.

The modern American woman is a political, environmental, and ecological menace. Consider the political candidates and causes she supports. A woman will vote for any political candidate who panders to her emotions, regardless of how morally depraved or intellectually vacuous that candidate is. Consider the bizarre and unstable personalities of the women who seek and often get elected to political offices. Consider a woman's shopping addictions and her insatiable appetite for worthless crap. Almost any item that glitters, has pretty colors, goes "ding" or has a silly slogan on it, will end up in her shopping cart. And if most of that worthless crap does not end up in her husband's garage or in a rented warehouse within a couple of months, it will end up in a landfill, never to be seen again until it shows up around the neck or in the intestinal tract of some poor suffering critter that was only foraging for food.

Ask any married man for a description of the worthless crap his wife collects (hoards.) It's maddening. If you doubt me or those men concerning the insatiable material appetites of women, do your own experiment. Pick any woman at random. Follow her for one week and watch what she buys in grocery stores, drug stores, and shopping malls. Monitor her mailbox and front door to log the deliveries by the postal service, UPS, and FedEx. Collect one week's worth of the garbage she places by the curb. Take it home, dump it out and itemize what you recover. Card board boxes, bubble envelopes, bubble wrap, plastic container, gift wrapping paper, half-full cosmetic containers, expired prescription and non-prescription medications, half-full containers of hazardous or potentially hazardous wastes such as insecticides, hairsprays, air fresheners, and disinfectants. Calculate the cubic volume and weight of those items. Then multiply those figures by one hundred million, the approximate number of adult females between twenty and seventy years-old in the US. You will then have an idea of the huge environmental and ecological impact women have.

I realize that experiment is not practical because it would take a team of investigators to carry it out. And you're probably thinking "Going through someone's garbage? That's disgusting!" To the contrary. It's a fascinating and valuable investigative tool. You can tell more about a person by what they consume and what they throw away than they will tell you about themselves, and certainly more than they want you to know. To make the experiment easier, use any adult female who you share a household with or whose home you have regular legal access to. The result will be pretty close to the same as it would be for a stranger.

Almost everything that a woman buys is bought on impulse, not out of need. Clicking the "Buy" icon on an internet shopping sight or sliding a credit card into a credit card reader at a store has nearly the same physiological and psychological effect on her as smoking crack cocaine or having an orgasm. If you want to infuriate an alcoholic or a drug addict, call them an alcoholic or a drug addict. If you want to infuriate a woman who is shopaholic or a hoarder, call her a shopaholic or a hoarder. The fact that the accusation can be substantiated by irrefutable evidence will not stop her from hating your guts for noticing it and pointing it out to her.

Not only are women environmental and ecological menaces, they are slobs. If you're a single man who doubts that statement, just ask any married or formerly married man. But you say "I've been inside women's homes and those homes have been neat and clean." Of course you have, and of course they were. She spent hours vacuuming, mopping and cleaning before you arrived so you wouldn't see that she was slob. You didn't look in her shower stall, in her closet, in her dresser drawers or under her bed where she hurriedly jammed all of the clutter that she allowed to accumulate during the previous two weeks. And you didn't look in her garbage can or washing machine to see the filthy rags she used to clean before you arrived. If she didn't personally do the cleaning, some other less fortunate woman did. That woman is called "the maid."

Here is another little investigative experiment you can do for your own amusement. Go to the parking lot of a typical supermarket, drug store, or shopping center. Look through the windows of any unoccupied car that belongs to a woman. You ask "How can I tell if a car belongs to a woman?" Here are a few clues to look for: Most women are shorter than men, so the driver's seat is usually adjusted close to the steering wheel. Stand behind the car approximately where the driver of another car would be at a traffic light behind the target car. Now look at the rear view mirror of the target car. If you don't see the driver's headrest or approximately where the driver's face should appear in the mirror, that means the last thing she did before getting out of the car was turn the mirror so she could see herself while applying lipstick or makeup. Some women drive around with their mirror in that position. There are few things a woman enjoys more than looking at herself in a mirror. Look for bumper stickers or window decals that support liberal political candidates and social causes, or that have silly slogans like "live, laugh, love" or "dance like nobody is watching." Look for beads, necklaces, dream catchers, religious icons or handcuffs hanging from the rear view mirror. Look for stuffed animals on the rear deck or dashboard. Look for windows that are clouded by the accumulation of cigarette smoke, hair spray, perfume, or other volatile organic compounds that were discharged, burned or evaporated within the passenger compartment. Look for dried bird excrement, tree sap or three month's worth of accumulated dirt on the exterior. Look for dents and chipped paint on the edges of the driver's door. Look for bumpers and air damns that are damaged from striking concrete parking curbs or other vehicles while pulling forward or backing. Look for wheels, tires, and rocker panels that are damaged from bad parallel parking attempts. Look for tires that are visibly low on air pressure. Once these exterior indicators make you suspect that the target vehicle belongs to a woman, turn your attention to the interior. Assuming you can see through the windows, here are a few things you are likely to notice: Makeup residue ground into the steering wheel, gear shift lever and upholstery. Cosmetic containers, compact discs, pieces of french fries, fast food bags, breath mints, gum wrappers, plastic eating utensils, straws, cigarette butts, store receipts, and an assortment of plastic and aluminum beverage containers on the floor, in the console or jammed between the seats. When you're certain the car belongs to a woman, park nearby and wait to see who walks or waddles out to it. I rest my case.

Numerous professional auto detailing technicians have posted videos of their work on YouTube. The filthiest of the cars they service belong to women. Months or years worth of candy, food, makeup and other filth is ground into the carping and upholstery. Sometimes the technician makes a reference to the customer's gender. When he doesn't, child's toys and women's cosmetics and clothing are a dead giveaway. It would probably have taken less then a minute for the woman to collect the trash and throw it away each time she got out of her car. Maybe another two minutes to wipe down the interior with one or two prepackaged cleaning wipes. But anything even remotely associated with janitorial services is beneath the dignity of the modern American "Princess." She deserves to ride in a chauffeur driven limousine with a nanny supervising her children. It's bad enough that she has to drive herself around in a six year-old sedan. She certainly isn't going to suffer the indignity of cleaning up behind her children, let alone herself. Here is a related anecdote:

A law enforcement investigator friend of mine was sitting in his unmarked car in the parking lot of a well known fast food restaurant. A woman in a 'soccer mom SUV' went through the drive-thru lane and ordered several "kids meals" that also contained promotional toys from a recently released fantasy movie for children. After receiving the meals, the woman drove into the parking lot, removed the toys from the bags, and threw the bags of food and beverages onto the parking lot before driving away.

HOW DID WE GET HERE?

"Men and women are made for each other, but their mutual dependence differs in degree; man is dependent on woman through his desires; woman is dependent on man through her desires and also her needs; he could do without her better than she can do without him. She cannot fulfill her purpose in life without his aid, without his goodwill, without his respect; she is dependent on our feelings, on the price we put upon her virtue, and the opinion we have of her charms and her deserts. Nature herself has decreed that woman, both for herself and her children, should be at the mercy of man's judgment." ~ Jean-Jacques Rousseau, 1712 – 1778, Genevan philosopher, highly influential in the development of modern political, economic and educational thought.

Never heard that quote before, did you? That truth infuriates modern women, and it is anathema to the feminized radical leftists in the news media, the entertainment industry, and educational institutions. To counter that truth, those radicals use a page from Adolph Hitler's playbook.

"If you tell a big enough lie and tell it frequently enough, it will be believed."

In the subsections that follow, I'll be showing you some of the ways and means by which those people and industries financially profit from your ideological enslavement and ignorance.

EDUCATION

After you were born, you cried when you were hungry or when you soiled yourself. It was almost certainly a woman who put a bottle in your mouth or changed your diaper. She did not do those things entirely out of love or out of concern for your hunger and discomfort. She did them to shut you up. And when she took you for those outdoor stroller rides that you can't even remember, it was because she wanted the fresh air and change of scenery for herself. You were only along for the ride.

When you were old enough to be left partially unattended, but were still in diapers, your mother plopped you on the floor in front of a television where your undeveloped mind was systematically corrupted by silly cartoons and commercials for sugary cereals and useless toys. While you sat there mesmerized, she talked or texted with friends, posted stupid comments and nearly nude pictures of herself on social media platforms, and checked her dating site accounts to see if anyone swiped right. When you were old enough, and if she could afford it, she put you in day care so she didn't have to deal with your inconvenient and annoying little self. Even married women who have husbands with good jobs often claim that they need to go back to work for income as an excuse to put their children in day care. They're lying. The cost of infant day care today is approximately $8,000 to $12,000 per year. If she has more than one child, the cost will double. Add to that the work related costs of fuel, vehicle maintenance or public transportation, work clothes, dining out, income tax, and other expenses associated with employment, what little she has left from her paycheck hardly offsets the cost of daycare unless she has a high paying job. And even then it doesn't offset the emotional damage a boy sustains when he consciously or subconsciously realizes that his mother cares more about her own personal agenda than she cares about him. And her agenda is to go back to the fun life she had before he came along and disrupted it.

If you were in day care, the people who took care of you were women. Those women had no particular affection for you. You were a paycheck. They either owned the business or they were employees who were hired for their availability, not for their intelligence, their moral character or their understanding of boys. Their job was to keep you alive and uninjured until your mother or whoever she designated could pick you up in the afternoon. Until then, you were exposed to the spontaneous emotional eruptions and mindless prattle of the women at the daycare. And you, as a vulnerable child, absorbed whatever you were exposed to.

If you're an eighteen to fifty year-old man today who was raised by a single or divorced mother, you have no idea how much damage she did to you. Much of that damage can be repaired, but not until you acknowledge it exists and are willing to fix it. The first thing you need to do is understand that your mother was not your friend and she was not interested in your long term physical and mental health. If you were blessed with natural intelligence, good looks and athletic abilities, your mother used you as a fashion accessory and a conversation piece to impress her friends. If you weren't so mentally, aesthetically and athletically gifted, she didn't try to help you make the most of what you had. She tried to turn you into an emotional and psychological cripple like herself. I'm sorry if that stings. But take a few minutes to objectively examine how mommy deals with life. Does she take credit for good things that other people accomplish? Does she exaggerate or lie about her own accomplishments and abilities? Does she take responsibility for the problems she creates in her life? Or does she constantly make excuses and blame other people for them? People like your father, her father, her mother, her boss or former boss, etc. Then ask yourself if you are following those same behavior patterns. Be honest with yourself. If the answer is yes and you can admit it, you've taken the first giant step towards overcoming it.

Now, back to your infancy. As you began to explore the world around you as a toddler, the most common communication you had from your mother was "NO!" or "STOP THAT!" or "DON'T TOUCH THAT!" Your failure to comply probably resulted in a swat on the backside instead of an explanation as to why the thing you were doing was wrong. She couldn't give you an explanation because she didn't have one. She just knew that it was annoying her. The swat instilled fear of punishment and humiliation that compelled you to obediently do and believe whatever she told you. By the time you developed critical thinking skills and could rationally decipher what was true or false, right or wrong, or in your best interest, your fear of punishment and humiliation or your fear of not pleasing mommy was so deeply ingrained in your subconscious mind that it overrides your will to exercise your independence and critical thinking.

When you were old enough to enter the public school system, most or all of your elementary school teachers were women. The atmosphere in middle school was very much like that of elementary school. High School was probably a slight improvement. If there was a man worthy of your respect at any of those schools, the sign on his office door said "Coach" or "Custodian." There might have been a few male teachers who were potentially good role models. But they had to keep a low profile. Almost any display of genuine masculinity could get a man fired.

If you doubt what I'm telling you, check it out for yourself. Go to any public school's internet website and look at the roster of administrators and teachers. Calculate the ratio of females to males. Many of those sites have individual or group photographs of the staff. Look closely at those photos. How many of those women are obese? How many of them are showing some cleavage? How many of them have a look on their face that says "bat-shit-crazy"? Teaching is a noble profession. But all too often today's classrooms are laboratories, school administrators and teachers are mad scientists, and students are guinea pigs used to test toxic philosophical, political, and social viruses on. And parents wonder why their kid's behavioral problems go into overdrive about the same time those kids start going to public schools.

Most women teachers lean heavily toward the liberal side of the political / philosophical / social spectrum. An impressionable male child who spends seven hours a day, one-hundred and eighty days out of the year, for twelve years, under the direct authority and influence of obese, bat-shit-crazy liberal women, will probably become an obese, bat-shit-crazy liberal young man. That will not enhance his prospects of having secure employment, stable relationships, or an otherwise healthy and productive life.

Approximately fifty percent of college professors today are women. Most of those women have radical feminist social and political views. A man who attends college and has female professors who teache STEM related subjects (science, technology, engineering, math), is probably safe. Those subjects are based on objective sciences. But if the subject is philosophical or theoretical in nature, such as any of the political or social sciences, he could have a problem if he does not worship at the professor's alter.

The objective of modern so-called "institutions of higher learning" is not to provide men with knowledge and skills that are practical and useful to them as men. It is to philosophically indoctrinate them and turn them into drones who will mindlessly service the hives in a radically feminized society.

Most of you are too young to remember this, but there was a time in America when there were men only environments; organizations and social clubs that only men could be members of. Boy scouts, all male boarding schools, little league ball teams, etc. were places where boys could interact, bond, and learn about team work under the guidance of responsible men, without having to worry about offending women or being accused of "inappropriate behavior." If boys behaved inappropriately, the men supervising them knew how to deal with it, man to little man. Interacting with other males without having to listen to whining or snide criticism from women was so satisfying that, when they became men, they formed or joined "Men's Clubs" that restricted membership to men only.

Women hated this "men only" stuff because they weren't in control of it. So they filed discrimination law suits in courts and petitioned legislatures to pass laws that gave them access to those male only spaces. And, not surprisingly, feminist and pansy judges and legislators gave them the control they wanted. Men's clubs were destroyed and men were stripped of their natural born right to choose their friends and associates without having to explain or justify it to anyone. Women simply cannot stand the thought of men not wanting to be in their presence or under their control.

THERE'S NO PLACE LIKE HOME

When you weren't at day care or school, you were probably at home with a single mother who tried to control everything and everyone around her. That's probably why your father couldn't stand living with her for more than a few months or a couple of years at the most after you were born. Unfortunately for you, she got custody and you became her "little man" and a captive audience. Who controlled the radio, television, printed media, thermostat, meals, etc. in your house? Did the thermostat go up and down like a yo-yo because mommy was having "hot flashes"? Did mommy seem to go crazy for no apparent reason for a week or so about the same time every month? Was the television always tuned to romance movies, shopping networks, or talk shows hosted by screeching women who all talked at the same time? Did the magazines in your home have titles like Cosmopolitan, Vanity Fair, and Vogue? Was the radio tuned to stations overloaded with tattooed sluts posing as "musical artists"? You know who I'm talking about.

Let me take a brief detour on the subject of music. The music and lyrics produced by the modern music industry is mindless rubbish. A large percentage of the celebrities in the music industry are one or more of the following: sociopaths, narcissists, drug addicts, alcoholics, convicted criminals, or frequent fliers at drug rehab centers, psychiatric clinics, or county jails. And yet these celebrities are the people that your mother admired, imitated, and exposed you to. Try as you may, you cannot disassociate the music from the celebrities who produce and perform it. And the magazines and talk shows that appealed to your mother promoted these celebrities as people to be admired and applauded.

So, what is my point about the modern music industry? For the listener, music is like the alcohol in liquid medications. That alcohol has no medicinal value. It is there as a preservative and solvent that keeps the active ingredients from degrading or separating from the carrier solution. A catchy tune and rhythm can be remembered without lyrics. But if it has lyrics, it is doubtful that you will be able to hum the tune without taping your foot and thinking or singing the lyrics. If those lyrics carry unhealthy ideas or imagery, those ideas and images will become part of your mental programming. Once they are, it is difficult to delete them. Another well known quote from The Mourning Bride by William Congreve is "Music hath charms to soothe a savage breast. To soften Rocks, or bend a knotted Oak." If that is true, and I believe that it is, then music can also have counter charms that incite anger, violence, licentiousness, and general stupidity. Music has the power to carry the beliefs expressed in lyrics into your brain while bypassing your analytical faculties. And most of the beliefs and images associated with today's music only serve to weaken the intellect and willpower of men.

A guest blog posted in Scientific American in October of 2012 was titled "The Power of Music: Mind Control by Rhythmic Sound." It was written by R. Douglas Fields. It is a must read.

Doctor Fields is a brilliant neuroscientist and an international authority on brain development and the cellular mechanisms of memory. The blog quotes other authoritative sources as well. The bottom line is that music has a far more powerful effect on human emotions and behavior than people are aware of.

TELEVISION NEWS

Search YouTube for video clips of network news broadcasts from the late fifties to early seventies. Nearly all of the anchors were men. Chet Huntley, David Brinkley, Frank Reynolds and many of their contemporaries typified the stoic demeanor and elocutionary skills of the news professionals of their day. Most of the television news professionals of today are women who sound more like game show contestants than professional broadcasters. The rapidly shrinking number of male news professionals today are only deeper-voiced androgynous versions of the women. The women news anchors and reporters are mostly political leftists and wannabe actresses who are fighting losing battles against weight gain and wrinkles. Tons of makeup, stylish fashions, figure altering undergarments, strategic lighting and directors who make sure the cameras don't zoom in too closely will usually keep you from noticing. The younger female reporters who are still relatively hot and fresh out of journalism school are hired as field reporters or weekend anchors. Do you honestly believe any of these women were hired for their analytical or elocutionary skills? Duh! They were hired to fill gender quotas or because they looked good. Station managers know that dimwitted heterosexual men will watch a good looking female anchor or reporter for that reason alone. When the broadcast is over, you won't remember much of what she said. But you will remember her pretty eyes, her sensual lips, her form fitting attire and whatever happened to be standing out on it. The station manager doesn't care and neither does she. The station manager wants good ratings. And she enjoys the ego boost she gets from the lurid fan mail sent to her by psychotic men telling her in graphic detail what they would like to do to her. Shocking? Not really. "Fifty Shades of Gray", a fictional novel about sexual sadomasochism and bondage, sold 15.2 million copies from 2010 through 2019. I think you would be hard pressed to find many men who bought or read that book. I think you would be equally hard pressed to find many woman who did not. You can probably find a copy of it (along with a vibrating sex toy) in the nightstand of million of American women, including at least a few female television news anchors and reporters who would consider you a pig and a pervert for looking at a Playboy or Hustler magazine.

In 1982, Don Henley and Danny Kortchmar wrote a song that is perhaps the most concise, accurate and entertaining description of the modern television news media that you will ever hear. If you haven't heard it, I highly recommend it. The title is "Dirty Laundry."

ADVERTISING AND ENTERTAINMENT

As if the minefields of bad parenting, bad education, bad music, and bad news media were not bad enough, the entertainment and advertising industries have made things many times worse. Nearly twenty four hours a day, men are emotionally and psychologically bludgeoned by sitcoms, dramas, movies, commercials and print advertisements that portray men as either violent sociopaths or spineless idiots who can't change a diaper, mop a floor, or make a meal without it turning into a disaster. These assaults have been so unrelenting for so long that men have become desensitized to it and accept these warped representations of manhood as normal healthy traits to be imitated. Or, as Joseph Goebbels, Adolph Hitler's minister of propaganda, so succinctly put it: "If you tell a lie big enough and keep repeating it, people will eventually come to believe it. The lie can be maintained only for such time as the State can shield the people from the political, economic and/or military consequences of the lie. It thus becomes vitally important for the State to use all of its powers to repress dissent, for the truth is the mortal enemy of the lie, and thus by extension, the truth is the greatest enemy of the State."

In 2015, BMW ran a television commercial for its X1 sport utility vehicle. The driver was an attractive and well-put-together young woman. She backed the SUV into the driveway of an upper class residence at a high rate of speed with the rear cargo door open. A timid looking young man about the same age stood in the driveway directly in the path of the SUV. When the SUV was dangerously close to the man, the woman slammed on the brakes. The cargo area full of the man's personal belongings were unceremoniously catapulted from the cargo area and onto the driveway at the man's feet. The man just stood there looking like a confused child as the woman drove away with a self-satisfied smirk on her face. The man, seeing his neighbor watching these events, shouts "It's complicated. She's just dropping off my stuff." BMW ran the same ad in 2019 for the same vehicle as preowned. Who do you think the target audience was for that commercial? Advertising executives know that publicly treating a man with ridicule and contempt has enormous appeal to modern women. There are many other corporations that use similar advertising tactics to entice women into buying their products. A more realistic and satisfying ending to that BMW commercial would have been for the man to pull the woman out through the driver's window and throttle her senseless before she could drive away.

Here's a more gender neutral example of how the advertising industry's manipulation techniques work. Closely watch the next prescription medicine commercial you see on television. When it gets to the part where the narrator starts listing all of the possible negative side effects, pay close attention to his or her voice, the music and the images. His or her voice voice and delivery will be soft and pleasant. The background music will be in a major key or an upbeat time signature that evokes happiness and confidence. The video images will be in slow motion, showing people laughing or smiling in some romantic or fun recreational activity. All three of those elements are inconsistent with the message that the medicine being advertised could kill you. But people will naturally associate the pleasant voice, upbeat music and happy images with a favorable outcome rather than death.

In nearly every advertisement that you see, the images, the music and the message will have a troubling dissonance when compared to the real world performance of the product being sold. Cars, trucks, beer, toothpaste, bread, women, etc. And yes, women are a product that the advertising and entertainment industry is constantly trying to sell to witless men. You would not be very far off base if you thought of those industries as little more than corporate pimps.

If you were extremely thirsty and you found a bottle containing a clear liquid, you would not drink that liquid without reading the label. If it had no label, you would first sniff the contents. If it had no distinguishable aroma and you were smart, you would take a small sip make sure it was safe before you gulped down the rest of it. But when you watch advertisements, television and movies, you are unwittingly ingesting the messages that producers and advertisers want you to consume without objectively evaluating the accuracy of the messages or the toxicity of the products. If you eat something fattening that upsets your stomach, you can go for a long walk and take an antacid to deal with the calories and indigestion. But the ideological excrement that corporations and social engineers are pumping into your brain in mass quantities every day by advertising, movies and television programs is much more toxic and much more difficult to purge from your system than anything handed to you in a paper bag from a fast-food drive-thru window.

Lest you think these are just my half-baked opinions, I would refer you to a well researched book on the subject. The book is "The Hidden Persuaders" by Vance Packard. It was originally published in 1957. But in light of the major advances in audio and video technology since then, it is even more relevant today than it was when it was published. It's a must read and is available from Amazon. The New Yorker magazine describes it as "A brisk, authoritative and frightening report on how manufacturers, fundraisers and politicians are attempting to turn the American mind into a kind of catatonic dough that will buy, give or vote at their command."

I don't care how smart you think you are, you are not immune. Neither am I. In doing the research for this book, I made it a point to spend a few minutes mentally preparing before immersing myself into the cesspools that I'm warning you about. And I limited my exposure time during each session.

Between home, school, news media, entertainment and advertisements, the first eighteen years of your brain was programmed to accept and conform to social and cultural conventions that are geared toward breaking down your resistance, psychologically emasculating you, and making you an unwitting slave. And women are the primary tool used to accomplish that via your natural sexual attraction to them. Do you honestly think that has been beneficial to your physical and mental health? Has it helped you achieve your goals, become a more noble human being, or navigate the white water rapids of everyday life? The 1999 movie "The Matrix" is a superb metaphor for what has been done to you. And like the character "Neo" before he was unplugged from the Matrix, you aren't even aware of it.

Women too have been victims of the same systems that prey upon the weaknesses of men.

From the time they are little girls, women are raised to believe they are princesses whose most valuable asset is their beauty and sexuality. Consider the mothers who makeup and dress their innocent prepubescent little girls to look and act like whores, and then enter them in so-called "beauty pageants" and "talent contests." How do you think these little girls will behave when they grow up? Like narcissistic whores, of course. Think of the pretty little girls that Disney and other entertainment giants groomed as child "stars" who today are mentally ill adult drug addicts and alcoholics. And the parents who allowed or facilitated this happening right under their noses refuse to acknowledge their culpability for destroying the lives of their children.

Cosmopolitan magazine, or "Cosmo" as it is often called, is the world's number one selling women's magazine. A man need not read its nauseating contents to discover just how warped modern women have become. The photos and article titles on the covers are enough to cause a thinking man to projectile vomit. I did a Google image search for Cosmopolitan magazine covers. You can do the same. In addition to photos of shamelessly clad female celebrities, here are just a few of the article titles that appeared on the covers of a few past issues:

- "Kinky ideas to try in bed"
- "How to scam your boss"
- "Trick your boss into giving you a raise"
- "Cheating is about to be easier than ever"
- "Simple ways to make him worship you"
- "Sex tips so hot you'll get turned on just reading them"
- "Look hotter naked"
- "5 Ways to keep lust alive"
- "Make him beg for it!"
- How to fire up his desire in bed"
- "Sex tricks he's never seen before"
- "See how these real women snagged hunky celeb husbands"

The obvious implication is that women do not view men as human beings worthy of respect, but rather as tools to be controlled and manipulated for personal gain and gratification. Based on Cosmo's ubiquitous presence, the woman who raised you or the woman that you are considering as a potential wife probably consumed most of her philosophical meals at Cosmo's hog trough or in some comparable pigpen.

HALLMARK

The Hallmark Channel is just one of several American television cable channels whose content appeals almost exclusively to women whose emotional development stopped somewhere between their eighth and sixteenth birthdays. That arrested emotional development has enabled movie studios and writers to make enormous profits by producing modern ripoffs of fairy tales like Snow White, Sleeping Beauty, and Cinderella. In these modern ripoffs, the protagonist woman is a smart and pretty business owner or media personality. Instead of an evil princess, wicked witch or abusive stepmother, the villain is an abusive and unattractive man in the form of a boss, a coworker or an ex-husband. The hero is a handsome and wealthy corporate executive or an actual prince who travels around in a private jet and a chauffeured limousine, and who lives in a fifteen-thousand square foot Beverly Hills mansion or an actual palace. The plot begins with the woman being taken advantage of or abused in some way by the villain. The woman meets the hero who falls in love with her. The story ends with the hero rescuing the damsel in distress. The villain suffers multiple calamities for his wickedness while the hero and the damsel implicitly live happily ever after. Everything in-between the beginning and ending are absurd scenarios that have an undercurrent of sexual tension. In other words, it's all bullshit that has nothing to do with reality. But women eat that crap up like chocolate ice cream. Most of those women are so emotionally retarded that they think this fairy tale is within their reach. When they fail to make it their reality, they attempt to alleviate their misery by impulse shopping for things they don't need and can't afford, or by consuming copious amounts of antidepressants and alcohol. Many, if not most of them, will spend what is left of their life in counseling and rehab before dying miserable and lonely old women.

To the horrible detriment of the physical and mental health of women, these absurd fantasies implicitly or explicitly suggest that they are potential realities. An advertisement for a reality program on a different network parades a half-dozen morbidly obese women in front of the camera and describes them as voluptuous, curvy, bombshell, size sexy. The host of the program is billed elsewhere as one of Hollywood's hottest celebrity stylists who helps women tap into the perfect fashion formula. A man who truly cared about the mental and physical well-being of women would, as compassionately as possible, encourage them to get a grip on reality and get the physical and psychological help they desperately need, instead of exploiting the ugliest part of their nature; their vanity. The reality is that no amount of makeup or stylish clothing can make a morbidly obese woman into a voluptuous, curvy, bombshell. All it can do is make her look ridiculous, pathetic, or grotesque.

If you marry a modern woman, you'd better prepare yourself to deal with this delusional nonsense. If she gains fifty pounds of fat and another fifty pounds of bad attitude, she will still expect you to treat her like a movie princess. She will expect you to become romantically aroused instead of nauseated when she lumbers into the bedroom looking like a hippopotamus in a see-through nightie. Because of the brainwashing you have undergone for your entire life up to that point, there is a strong possibility that you, without even realizing it, will revert to your default programming. You'll cave in to her expectations to avoid hurting her feelings and having to listen to her cry about how uncaring and insensitive you are to her emotional needs. This conflict between your natural visceral reaction and your brainwashed programming has the potential to psychologically rip you apart. But she won't care. From her perspective, your only purpose in life is to make her happy and validate her existence, on her terms.

HOLIDAY NIGHTMARES

Corporate powers have ordained several woman-worshiping holidays during the year. Anniversaries, birthdays, Valentine's day and Mother's day are a few of them. Corporations and their advertisers have brainwashed you into believing that you have a moral obligation to buy their products as gifts for your wife in recognition of the holiday, even if you have to take out a personal loan or sell your most cherished possessions to afford it. And heaven help you if you don't. One of my clients told me that he forgot to buy his fifty-five year-old wife a Valentine card one year after twenty years of marriage. She didn't speak to him for nearly a week. He said that would have been fine with him if she had not passive-aggressively stomped around their house like an angry eight year-old with a scowl on her face for the entire time.

This kind of infantile passive-aggressive behavior by chronologically adult women is typical today. And our warped social and cultural systems validate it as acceptable. All of these holiday gifts that you are psychologically bullied into buying for women are nothing more than homage paid to a woman for having a vagina and a heartbeat. I recently saw a print advertisement for a flower shop that illustrates the point. The photo in the ad showed three separate and progressively larger bouquets of red roses. The first bouquet had about a dozen roses. The second was about twice that size, and the third was about twice the size of the second. Above the three bouquets was a bold red caption that asked "HOW MAD IS SHE?" Below the first bouquet was a caption that said "LATE FOR A DATE?" Below the second bouquet was "FORGOT THE ANNIVERSARY?" Below the third and largest bouquet was "ARRGH. . . FORGOT IT AGAIN?" The message is unmistakable. As a man, anything you do that upsets or offends a woman's selfish sense of entitlement and craving for attention is a sin for which you must do penance by giving her gifts. This idiotic scenario has been presented as humor in so many sitcoms, movies and advertisements, that men laugh and accept it as reasonable. Well, it isn't funny and it isn't reasonable. Stop laughing at it and stop caving into it!

Not long after seeing that flower shop

advertisement, I was having lunch at a popular local restaurant. On the wall beside my booth was a large tan poster with three large white dollar signs on it. In large black letters were the words "MEN, CHOCOLATE AND COFFEE ARE ALL BETTER RICH." Women find that amusing. As a man, how do you like having your human value decided by women based on how much money you have? How amused do you think women would be by a poster that had a picture of three slim and sexy twenty year-old women and the caption "WOMEN, VEAL AND LAMB ARE ALL BETTER YOUNG"? Do you think they would laugh at a poster showing a plump healthy pair of female breasts and the words "WOMEN, CHICKEN AND TURKEY ARE ALL BETTER WITH BIG BREASTS"? The comment about men being better rich isn't offensive or even surprising when you consider the mentality of the women who are amused by it.

THE MODERN CHURCH

"Woman – and the legends say it also – is the tool of the devil. She is generally stupid, but the devil lends her his brain when she works for him. Here you see, she has done miracles of thinking, far-sightedness, constancy, in order to do something nasty; but as soon as something not nasty is needed, she cannot understand the simplest thing; she cannot see farther than the present moment and there is no self-control and no patience. . ." - Leo Tolstoy, 1828 – 1910, from The Journal of Leo Tolstoy, first volume, translator Rose Strunsky.

Tolstoy's understanding of female nature was far superior to that of most modern church pastors. Perhaps the most dangerous brainwashing that is done to young men today is done by those pastors. An excellent example comes to mind. A senior pastor of a large neo-charismatic church in Texas also operates, along with his wife, what they call a Christian Marriage Ministry. I recently watched a video clip from what appeared to be one of his marriage seminars. The clip was only a minute long. Here is the transcript from that clip.

Pastor: "So this is a little thing I saw about romance, and it says how to win your spouse. How to be romantic in your spouses language. It says how to win your wife. How to be romantic to your wife. Dine her, call her, hug her, support her, hold her, surprise her, compliment her, smile at her, listen to her, laugh with her, cry with her, romance her, believe in her, cuddle with her, shop with her, give her jewelry, buy her flowers, hold her hand, write love letters to her, go to the end of the earth and back again for her. Here's how to win your husband: show up naked and bring food." [Pastor pauses while men and women in the audience laugh. As the laughter subsides, the pastor tags the end of the remarks with] "And the food is optional."

Messages like that are what young men are likely to hear in many post-modern churches today. It is usually just presented with a little less vulgarity. If you are a young man in a typical church today, you are either implicitly or explicitly told that you have divine obligations to marry; to put your wife on a pedestal; to meet her ridiculous expectations; and to carry her physical, emotional, psychological, and financial baggage until you are dead. Too many men think; "The pastor said it, so it must be right." So those men put themselves into an early grave by trying to meet the pastor's expectations.

The clearly implied message in the pastor's previously quoted comments is that men are little more than ignorant sex-crazed animals who place their carnal desires above every rational consideration. Those comments also do enormous harm to women by validating their natural fallen egocentric cravings to be dined, called, hugged, supported, complimented, smiled at, listened to, laughed with, cried with, romanced, believed, cuddled, shopped with, given jewelry and flowers, have her hand held, receive love letters and have a man go to the end of the earth and back for her. In other words, to be "Idolized." That proposition is all the more disgusting coming from the mouth of a man who claims to be a Christian pastor, especially in light of the explicit biblical condemnation of idolatry. And make no mistake; idolatry is precisely what he is promoting and what women want.

I would wager that most single or divorced women who claim to be "Christian" and show up at churches today are little more than secular anglers who see the church as the best fishing hole to catch a "good man." Their hook is baited with just enough carnality and worldliness to attract (or rather distract) an otherwise godly man's carnal attention, and just enough counterfeit piety to lull him into a false sense of security concerning her character and virtue. If you are a genuine Christian gent who allows yourself to be lured into proposing to one of these anglers, you can be reasonably certain that, after she says "I do" at the alter, she won't by the time the honeymoon is over. In fact, she will spend the rest of her life resisting your leadership and trying to manipulate you into kicking God off the throne of your heart and installing her in His place. And unless you can divorce her on biblical grounds, you will live and die a miserable man because she will never stop.

All of the things the aforementioned pastor told those men they should be doing for their wives are things that he can no doubt afford to to for his own wife. He's made a fortune fleecing his flock, selling books and putting on seminars. I suspect that many of the men who attend his seminars are so emotionally and financially stressed by trying to provide basic necessities to their families, they can barely afford to take their wives for anything more than occasional pizza, let alone buy her jewelry and flowers. Pastors today are either oblivious to or disinterested in the physical, emotional, and psychological welfare of the men in their congregations. It's all about pleasing the women. Why? Because women are the ones who drop their husband's money in the offering plate, buy "relationship" books (probably with their husbands' money), and then badger their husbands into taking them to the overpriced seminars associated with the books. Young Christian men often accept what pastors say because they want to 'do the right thing.' They assume pastors are telling them the truth. Those men are partially responsible for the misery that follows because they are too lazy to read the bible for themselves. Women accept what pastors say because it validates their selfish expectations. When their husbands fail to meet those expectations, those women rip off their masks of piety to reveal materialistic libidinous harpies who think they are justified in having their expectations met in another man's bed and billfold.

Pastors will sternly warn men in their congregations about the sin of 'looking on a woman to lust after her', and rightly so. But about the only thing those same pastors will say to a woman who shows up at a worship service looking like a hooker is "My, my! Don't you look nice this mornin!" as he wipes his spittle from the cover of his bible.

Pastors will tell the men in their congregations that they are on the verge of eternal damnation for looking at a magazine containing pictures of naked women. But those same pastors won't say a word to the women in their congregations who gorge themselves on literary pornography like "Fifty Shades Of Gray" and Harlequin Romance Novels.

I've heard several high profile pastors and self-proclaimed "Christian Psychologists" suggest that women who participate in the production of pornography are victims of the abusive men who control the pornography industry. That narrative is nonsense. The women who participate in the production of pornography are adults who do so willingly for profit, for pleasure, or some other thing that is of value to them at the time of their participation. It's only years later when they begin to feel guilty or are no longer attractive enough to be successful at it that they paint themselves as victims. Mistake me not! I'm not defending the pornography industry. It's a vile business that I wish would die from a lack of customers. I'm only pointing out that the women who participate in it are not victims. If they were victims, it's fair to wonder why so many professing "Christian" women who want to be viewed as virtuous go out of their way to wear makeup and clothing that would be more appropriate on a porn star or a prostitute than on a virtuous woman in a church sanctuary.

To keep young single men under their control, pastors will badger them about getting married. They say things like "You're not obeying God's will for your life if you don't marry and raise a family!" One of their favorite quotes to promote that proposition is the last few words of 1 Corinthians 7:9. And when they quote it, they do so with their best hellfire and brimstone delivery: "It is better to marry than to burn!" It is the height of arrogance for a pastor or any other man to tell another man what "God's will" is for that man's life when it comes to marriage.

Pastors should present the gospel. Getting married is not part of the gospel, and being married is not an evidence of or a requirement for salvation. It is an individual personal choice that each man has the God given right to make for himself. Furthermore, pastors tend to present the passage as an either / or proposition. They imply that having normal healthy sexual desire is the same as "burn." Well, it isn't! There is a third option. If a man finds the sight of an attractive woman sexually arousing, but he is capable of averting his eyes and focusing his attention elsewhere, that is not burning. If he just can't keep himself from looking at her, and he can't focus his mind on anything else because of it, that is burning. But here is the bad news for you gents in that second category. Getting married won't make the burning go away. To do that, you must overcome the root cause of it. And the root cause of it is your natural drives being unnaturally exacerbated by the unrelentingly assaults by the entertainment and advertising industries that I described earlier.

Telling a young man that he is in unconquerable bondage to his sexual drives and should marry because of it is dishonest and abusive because it just isn't so. A man who is momentarily aroused by a provocative advertisement or by an immodestly dressed woman who goes out of her way to flaunt herself at him has a choice. He can look away and think about something else. The arousal will go away on its own. And the more he practices that technique, the more effective it becomes and the more he will be able to focus on things that are truly important.

"Finally, brethren, whatsoever things are true, whatsoever things are honest, whatsoever things are just, whatsoever things are pure, whatsoever things are lovely, whatsoever things are of good report; if there be any virtue, and if there be any praise, think on these things." Philippians 4:8 KJV.

Modern pastors virtually ignore the devout man who earnestly desires a wife, but is unable to find a virtuous woman who is willing to marry him. Clichés like "Don't worry. There is someone out there for you" and "The right girl will come along" are unsupportable propositions that drive many men to despair. So why do pastors push marriage so hard at young men? I think there are several reasons, none of which are biblical or honorable.

1. Misery loves company. Many pastors are so miserable in their own marriages that the thought of a man finding spiritual peace and contentment in singleness bothers them. They want him to share in their marital misery. I can understand that to a degree. I've met quite a few pastors' wives. Spending more than a minute or two in the presence of most of those women was barely tolerable for me. It's hard to imagine what it must be like for the poor pastors who have to live with them.

2. Money. Women are more vulnerable than men when it comes to being fleeced. And when a man gets married, his money becomes her money. Remember; men have been brainwashed to please women. If they don't, they are subjected to guilt and shame by people around them or by their own internal programming. To get an idea of what this looks like, watch one of the well known so-called "Christian" television networks as their stylishly dressed and groomed 'name it and claim it / prosperity gospel' hucksters milks money from the studio and television audiences. When the camera pans the studio audience, you will see that the majority of audience members are women. Most of these

women wear an empty headed smile as they enthusiastically applaud whatever the hucksters say, regardless of how nonsensical and unbiblical it is. Meanwhile, their husband's sit quietly beside them with facial expressions consistent with dementia. But there they are; dutifully sitting with wives who, like most unbelieving women, couldn't care less about her husband's happiness as long as he keeps handing her his money.

3. Sex. Pastors who are waging a losing battle against their own carnal desires refuse to believe that every other man is not doing the same. It's a form of pride and envy. If the pastor doesn't have self-control, he assumes that other men can't have it either.

A man who is intellectually disciplined and spiritually illuminated can recognize the dangers of his own carnal desires and can navigate around them.

CHIVALRY

When I say the word "Chivalry", what image pops into your head? The story of Sir Walter Raleigh laying his cloak over a puddle so the Queen won't soil her feet? Knights defending the safety and honor of helpless damsels in distress? You might be surprised to know that

Chivalry, as an informal code of conduct, began to develop around 1200 AD. It covered a wide range of piety, honor, courage, manners, and nobility. It had very little to do with protecting women in particular. But by the time nineteenth and twentieth century American culture finished corrupting it, chivalry had become associated almost exclusively with men sacrificially serving women like slaves on some antebellum southern plantation.

Young boys are indoctrinated with the idea that they are supposed to protect women from harm, even at the cost of their own lives. They are told lies like "There is never a reason to hit a woman." Instead of being appreciative of the benefits that those sacrificial and protective services provide for them, modern women have turned it into an opportunity to exploit and abuse the men who provide them.

Smart men today have stopped being chivalrous toward women. And the women today who complain the most about chivalry being dead are the ones who brutally murdered it in each of its recurring incarnations by repeatedly stabbing it in the back or kicking it to death. Yes, chivalry is dead. Goodbye and good riddance to it. Any man who attempts to resuscitate it, resurrect it or clone it should be publicly flogged as a warning to other men.

TIPS FOR A BETTER LIFE

All that I have told you thus far would be of little value if I didn't offer you some concise tips for staying out of destructive entanglements with women. These tips are general, so you can alter them to fit your individual needs and circumstances. But do so with caution. Most of them have been successfully tested by other men. I suspect that many of you have been in the system for so long that it will be difficult for you to find your way out of it. Be patient. You didn't get there overnight, so don't expect to get out overnight. Take one step at a time, even if it is a small one. The slightest progress will be encouraging for you.

KNOW YOUR LIMITATIONS

"A good man always knows his limitations." Magnum Force, 1973, Dirty Harry to Lt. Briggs.

Sound advice from "Dirty" Harry Callahan. Physical injuries occur when people exceed their physical limitations. People exceed their limitations when they don't know what those limitations are. The same concept applies to emotional and psychological injuries. Spend some time honestly assessing your individual emotional and psychological limitations, and avoid exceeding them; especially where women are concerned. Do not use other men as a measure for your limitations. And do not become jealous or competitive with men who appear to have more success with women than you do. They won't look so successful to you in a couple of years when they're paying alimony and child support to their ex-wives, or being sued by women they knocked up, or being treated for a sexually transmitted disease, or being shot to death by the enraged husband or boyfriend of some woman they were screwing around with. Figure out what your natural gifts are and work on developing those gifts into useful and marketable skills that you can be proud of and that you can use to serve your fellow man. Your success will enable you to have a lifestyle that will attract women if you really want them. But when you discover the intrinsic value of your own life, you probably won't want them.

AVOID PORNOGRAPHY

"Sow a thought and you reap an action; sow an act and you reap a habit; sow a habit and you reap a character; sow a character and you reap a destiny." Ralph Waldo Emerson, 1803 – 1882,

American essayist, lecturer, philosopher, and poet.

Your sexual drive is your most serious vulnerability. Keep yourself aware that the social and cultural systems discussed earlier in this work will constantly be putting provocative images in front of you to try to make you stumble. Always remember that the people and companies that put those images in front of you are trying to break you down and control you by creating subconscious links between your natural response to the images and the products or services they sell. Find other things to occupy your mind. Go for a walk, pray, read a book, fly a kite, go fishing, or any one of a thousand other things that are more useful and satisfying than looking at images of women or thinking about them. The more you do that, the easier it will become and the more successful you will be.

BROMANCE VS ROMANCE

A "Bromance" is a close non-sexual relationship between men. Bromances are safer and more emotionally satisfying than the constant pressure and tension that are part and parcel of trying to please or entertain women. Establish friendships with men of good character that you share things in common with. A few hours with the guys restoring an old car; discussing religion or philosophy; tossing a football; shooting hoops; camping, fishing, playing poker, scuba or free diving, etc. is infinitely more satisfying than watching or listening to a woman cry during a romantic movie or listening to her gossip about the private lives of her friends and family members.

IGNORE INSULTS

The people who want you to share their misery or to be a slave on their plantation will use insults to try to manipulate you into going there. They might question your sexual orientation or your masculinity. Sometimes the insults will be phrased as subtle propositions like "You need a woman to be a fulfilled man." Or "If you don't have a wife, you'll die alone." Understand this: You don't need a woman to be a fulfilled man. And getting married is no guarantee that you won't die alone. It is far better to die alone and comfortable with the man that you are than it is to die alone because the woman who promised to be there for you until the end betrayed or abandoned you when you needed her the most. Worse still is dying in the presence of the woman who shortened your life by spending decades relentlessly sucking the life out of you. So, use your time and energy to become the man that you can call your friend when you greet him in the mirror each morning. Learn how to enjoy your life without sharing it with a woman. Once you achieve that, you can date or have relationships with women if you want to. If those relationships fall apart, you won't care because your self-esteem will not be dependent upon her affections for you.

BEWARE OF THE BAIT AND SWITCH

If a woman thinks you will be a good mule and provider for her, she will show interest in the things you like to do, even if she secretly hates them or has never done them before. Hunting, shooting, fishing, scuba diving, riding motorcycles, etc. She will pretend to enjoy those things to make you think she will be a terrific mate. When the honeymoon is over and she has you locked into the relationship, the things you like to do will be slowly and incrementally replaced by things she wants to do; dining out, shopping, watching romance movies, rearranging furniture, and a host of other things that will make you want to vomit. One day you'll wake up and say "What happened to my life?" Do not take the bait! How do you know whether or not a woman will do the bait and switch?

There is only one way to find out for sure. Do you really want to take that risk? Or as Dirty Harry would say; "Do ya feel lucky? Well, do ya, punk?"

AVOID SOCIAL MEDIA

If you use the internet, stay off of social media. The internet is fine if you are using it for professional research, educational purposes, catching up on news, email, paying bills, or similar time saving conveniences. Social media will waste your valuable time and drain your physical and mental energy. If you surf the internet, depending on your web browser, pictures of attractive women will appear in popup advertisements on your screen, frequently in the same general area. Tape a piece of paper over those areas, or wear a ball cap that lets you block the images from view with just a slight tilt of your head. Hone your reading skills. Stop looking at pictures unless those picture are technical diagrams or have some artistic / educational value. If you have magazines that contain advertisements that use pictures of attractive women as bait to get you to look at or buy the product being advertised, rip those advertisements out and toss them in the trash. You'll be amazed at how much space you will save in your magazine collection.

PREPARE FOR BATTLE

Before you leave you home, regardless of where you're going, remind yourself that there are going to be scores vain predatory women trolling for your attention. They won't necessarily want to date you, marry you, or have sex with you. They just want you to want to date, marry, or have sex with them. Your attention validates their existence. Those women will be heavily made up and / or provocatively dressed for that purpose. Settle it in you mind before you go that you will not look at them or interact with them any longer than is necessary. If you work in an office with women, arrange your desk or chair so you don't have to see them. If you go out to eat, pick a table or chair where you can sit with your back to them. Take reading or study material with you to keep yourself mentally occupied. Don't go to office parties and company picnics. And don't apologize for not going, or lie about the reason you aren't going. If someones asks why you aren't going, just say "Because I don't want to." If they ask why you don't want to, tell them that you have personal reasons that you don't care to discuss.

AVOID ALCOHOL

"I would not put a thief in my mouth to steal my brains." - Mattie Ross, "True Grit" by Charles Portis.

In the novel "True Grit", fourteen year-old Mattie Ross hires aging and hard drinking marshal "Rooster" Cogburn to track down the man who murdered her father. While camping for the night, Rooster gets drunk and Mattie expresses her disgust. In an effort to shut her up, Rooster offers her a drink of whiskey. She replies "I would not put a thief in my mouth to steal my brains." Mattie's reply was a paraphrase of a line from Shakespeare's "Othello" where Cassio laments; "Oh, that men should put an enemy in their mouths to steal away their brains! That we should, with joy, pleasance revel and applause, transform ourselves into beasts!" Mattie, Rooster, and Cassio are fictional characters. Lucius Annaeus Seneca, c 4 BC – c 65 AD, was a very real, very wise and highly respected Roman Stoic philosopher, statesman, and dramatist. Here is what he had to say on the subject:

"Drunkenness is nothing but a condition of insanity purposely assumed. . . Think of the calamities caused by drunkenness in a nation. This evil has betrayed to their enemies the most spirited and warlike races; this evil has made breaches in walls defended by the stubborn warfare of many years; this evil has forced under alien sway peoples who were utterly unyielding and defiant of the yoke; this evil has conquered by the wine-cup those who in the field were invincible."

In our own day, think of the people killed or injured in alcohol related automobile crashes, boating mishaps, industrial accidents, and recreational activities. Think of the fortunes lost, families broken, and health destroyed. But alcohol manufacturers want you to drink as much of their product as possible. Their advertisements are designed to manipulate you into linking their product to your masculinity and popularity. The tag line "Drink Responsibly" that is heard or printed at the end of those advertisements is nothing but shallow virtue signaling to try to make you think they care about your well-being. They don't. They only care about what's in your wallet. When you're dying of liver disease because of alcohol, you will have a hard time finding a doctor who who is willing to transplant the healthy liver of a recently deceased donor into the abdominal cavity of an alcoholic. A large percentage of domestic violence and homicide cases are alcohol related in the sense that the victim, assailant or both, were impaired by alcohol. If you find yourself in jail for DUI, vehicular homicide, domestic battery or some other criminal act because you were physically or mentally impaired by alcohol, it will not be the CEO of a beverage manufacturer or an advertising agency who pays your medical bills, posts your bond, pays your attorney or serves your prison sentence. But you say "I'm not an alcoholic!" That's what everyone who now attends Alcoholics Anonymous meetings used to say.

Here is a little piece of history you might find interesting. On April 15th, 1865, at approximately 9:00 pm, President Abraham Lincoln was attending a play at Ford's Theater in Washington, DC. John Parker was a DC police officer who was assigned to the post outside Lincoln's private box to protect the President. During intermission, Parker joined the footman and coachman of Lincoln's carriage for drinks in the Star Saloon next door to Ford's Theatre. When John Wilkes Booth entered the theater around 10:00 pm and crept up to the door to Lincoln's box, Parker's chair was empty. It isn't clear where Parker was when Booth pulled the trigger. But there is good reason to believe that he was still at the saloon. Parker had a history of drunkenness, including being drunk while on duty. His legacy is a dead president and an unmarked grave.

TAKE CARE OF YOUR HEALTH

"To keep the body in good health is a duty... otherwise we shall not be able to keep the mind strong and clear." – Buddha "It is health that is the real wealth, and not pieces of gold and silver." – Mahatma Gandhi

If you were not genetically endowed with great natural physical and intellectual abilities, that does not mean that you cannot make the most of what you were born with. If you develop sensible exercise, dietary and study habits, you can become a physical and mental force worthy of respect. Spending your time trying to make a woman happy will consume the time that you have to improve yourself, and it will corrode the physical and mental health that you already have.

CHOOSE YOUR FRIENDS WISELY

"Associate yourself with men of good quality if you esteem your own reputation; for 'tis better to be alone than in bad company." - George

Washington, 1732 – 1799.

"Do not be deceived. Bad company corrupts good morals." 1 Corinthians 15:33, NASB

Propositions like those occur so often, in so many different languages, and in such a wide variety of religious and philosophical contexts throughout history, you would be foolish to ignore them. The people you associate with will have a profound influence on the kind of person you are and how you behave. How do you determine who "men of good quality" are and what "bad company" is? It's not difficult. Men who encourage you when you do well, constructively criticize you when you do not, and who live lives that are consistent with the high values that they profess are men of good quality. Anyone who tries to compel or lure you into doing something illegal or that your conscience or common sense tells you is wrong is bad company. This is especially important for you to keep in mind when dealing with women, for several reasons. Your natural physical and emotional responses to an attractive woman can seriously cloud or distort your judgment. Women are always looking for ways to distract or confuse you, and then exploit your distraction and confusion for their own selfish purposes. As a general rule, a woman will not do anything for you or give anything to you unless she is trying to get something of greater value from you in return. If you keep that simple proposition in your mind the entire time your are dealing with women, you will probably be safe.

AVOID STARING AT WOMEN

Women claim to be annoyed by men staring at them. And yet they go out of their way to dress and behave in ways that they know will attract male attention. When a woman walks into wherever you happen to be, you'll probably notice her. That doesn't mean you have to stare at her, regardless of how good looking she might be. A wise man once said; "No matter how good she looks to you right now, some man somewhere is tired of putting up with her bullshit." By staring, you are giving her what she wants: Your attention and a reason to mock you. It's a form of control. If she is with another man at the time, she might also be trying start a cock fight over her. By staring at women you are neglecting giving your attention to yourself and the things that will make you a wiser and more noble person.

AVOID TALKING TO WOMEN

Do not speak to women unless they speak to you first. If they speak to you first, carefully listen to what they say and how they say it so you can construct an appropriate response if a response is even warranted. There is usually nothing of value to be gained by having more conversation with a woman than is absolutely necessary. Necessary conversations include daily commercial interaction with food service workers, cashiers, bank tellers, medical professionals, etc. Discussing politics, philosophy, economics, religion, movies, food, fashion, feelings, relationships, etc. with women is more than unnecessary. It is potentially destructive. If you spend enough time talking with a woman, one of two things will happen. You'll either become annoyed and experience a dangerous spike in your blood pressure. Or, without even realizing it, you'll start thinking, talking and behaving like a woman.

CHECK HER OUT
BEFORE TAKING HER OUT

Some of you may not have the willpower to resist dating or marrying. I understand that and I would not criticize you for it. But you don't have to be stupid about it. Background investigations are relatively inexpensive and will tell you things about your date or your future ex-wife that she will not tell you about herself. As numerous sages herein have already mentioned, it is a woman's nature to deceive. A background check is a good way to find out what a woman is hiding from you and how potentially dangerous she might be to you in a relationship. Doing a proper background investigation is a skill that takes time, training, and experience to hone. If you don't have those things, you're much better off hiring an experienced professional than trying to do it yourself. An experienced professional can see little details that could be major red flags that you would not notice. Even if it costs a couple of hundred dollars, it's money well spent. It can prevent you from wasting your time and money on someone who isn't worth it. It's cheaper than having a woman gut you like a fish in family court. And it's less painful than having her leave you to die on the side of a rural roadway.

PRENUPTIAL AGREEMENTS

If you meet a woman that you just can't resist wanting to marry, a legally binding prenuptial contract is a must. Just the suggestion of a prenup will be enough to make most women angrily terminate the relationship. If she is still willing to marry you and sign a prenup, you're not out of the woods. As long as you are married to her, you will need to monitor her behavior for signs of mental illness and monitor your assets to make sure that she isn't secretly siphoning them off.

LIFE INSURANCE

Do not name a woman as the beneficiary in a life insurance policy, even if she is your wife. Knowing that she can obtain wealth by your death is a strong motivation for her to kill you. If you are genuinely concerned about her welfare if something should happen to you, talk to an attorney about setting up a trust that the insurance benefit could be paid into, and then name a trusted male friend or associate as the executor who can control the disbursement of funds on a legitimate as-needed basis. Killing you for big lump sum payout is too much temptation for many modern women. Knowing that she can only get what she needs a little bit at a time might reduce her motivation.

RAINY DAY INSURANCE

From the moment you marry, you should have a plan to regularly save and hide money or other assets that can be converted to cash if needed. When I say hide, I mean put somewhere that only you know about and that she does not have access to. No matter how blissful your marriage seems on any particular day, that can change overnight. If it does, she will not be looking for an equitable settlement. She will be looking for the most cutthroat lawyer she can find and will try to leave you penniless. If you have not hidden some cash and assets, you could find yourself sleeping on friends sofa or living in your parent's basement. Consult a financial advisor. Better still, consult a private investigator who can tell you the dirty tricks to hide assets.

BIRTH CONTROL

Whether or not to have children is a personal choice that you and your future wife should firmly agree upon before you marry. And make sure that agreement is specified somewhere in the prenuptial contract. If the two of you agree that you don't want children, you'll have to agree on the method of birth control. If you opt for a vasectomy and she objects, she just showed her cards. She is already planning to change her mind. You just don't know when, and she isn't going to tell you. You might want to reassess your marriage plans. If you still want to marry her because she says that she will take responsibilities for birth control, you should get a vasectomy anyway and don't tell her about it. Women are infamously fickle. It's not even a debatable subject. How many times have you heard the cliché; "It's a woman's prerogative to change her mind!"? She will not care if her capricious change of mind destroys your long range plans and throws your life into total chaos. And what could create more chaos in your life than your wife having a child that you did not want, plan on, or expect. The fact that she lied to you and intentionally broke her agreement with you is meaningless to her because you are meaningless to her. But you will still be held responsible. Giving a woman that kind of destructive power over your future is extremely dangerous.

AUDIO AND VIDEO RECORDING

Disclaimer: It is generally against the law to audio / video record someone without their knowledge or consent under circumstance where they have a reasonable expectation of privacy. If you ignore this warning, you do so at your own risk.

As mentioned at the beginning of this book, false allegations of rape and battery have become almost epidemic. In spite of the accused men denying those allegations, the general attitude of society is that men are guilty until proven innocent. About the only thing that can prove his innocence is a video or audio recording that contradicts the allegation. Even corroborating male witnesses will be of limited value since it will be assumed that they are lying to protect the accused man. If you are going to allow a woman into your home, you'd better have an audio and video recording system in it, and make sure she knows it is there before you let her inside. But don't give her any other information about the system. If she asks you to turn the system off, tell her "No." If she insists, tell her to leave.

BE AFRAID OF THE DARK

If you are going to date a woman, always go to public places that have cameras. Be very careful about going to dark or secluded places. Use caution if you're going to ride with a woman in her car. Do not allow a woman to ride with you in your car unless you have a working dashcam with audio, and make sure that she is aware of.

AVOID FALSE RAPE ALLEGATIONS

False rape allegations are not as new as you

might think. Of the rape allegations I investigated as a police office, I would estimate that only twenty to thirty percent of those allegations were genuine rapes. The other seventy to eighty percent fell into one of the following the categories:

- Failure to pay rape
- Remorse rape
- Gross stupidity rape

Failure to pay rape is when a woman has consensual sex with a man in exchange for some form of payment, and the man refuses to pay after services are rendered. Here is a hypothetical scenario. You meet a woman in a casino. You buy her a few drinks and give her fifty dollars for the slot machines. She invites you back to her room and offers to have sex with you. You accept her offer. Afterwards she tells you to give her two hundred dollars more for the slots. You refuse. She says she will accuse you of raping her if you don't. You refuse and you leave her room. She calls the police and reports the incident accurately accept for you giving her money and what went on in her room. She will say that the two of you were having such a thought provoking discussion in the casino about the literary works of Ernest Hemingway that she invited you in to continue the discussion in her room, but that you held her down and raped her when she let you in. You're going to jail. And the only evidence needed to send you to prison for a substantial part of your life are any of your bodily fluids and her accusation. Proof beyond a reasonable doubt is not needed to convict a man of rape. He is presumed guilty unless he can prove his innocence. If all you have is your claim that the encounter was consensual, you're in trouble.

Remorse rape is when a woman has consensual sex with a man, but regrets doing so after thinking about it for an unspecified period of time from a few minutes to several years. There could be a number of reasons for her remorse. She might become pregnant and have no reasonable explanation to give to her husband or boyfriend. She might contract a sexually transmitted disease and have no reasonable explanation. Someone she knows might have unexpectedly seen her in a compromising position, and saying she was raped might be her only way out of embarrassment or divorce. You might have come into a large sum of money and she wants a piece of it. She has a political agenda. She wants her thirty minutes of fame. The amount of time that passes between her consensual sexual encounter and her reporting that she was raped are irrelevant. From the moment she accuses you, you will be on the defensive. Even if she cannot have you successfully prosecuted in criminal court, you will still be guilty in the court of public opinion. Her husband, male family members, or male friends might try to retaliate against you for something you didn't do.

Gross stupidity rape is when a woman intentionally puts herself into circumstances that she knew or should have known would place her in jeopardy of being raped. An anecdote from a past investigation comes to mind. At 11pm, the alleged victim was hitchhiking to our city from a city about ten miles away. The road she was hitchhiking on was an unlit lightly traveled rural highway. A car stopped to pick her up. It was occupied by three black males and two black females that she did not know. When she got into the car, they told her they were on their way to a party and asked her if she wanted to go with them. She said yes. They arrived at a house where a party was in progress. She consumed an unknown quantity of alcohol and smoked some weed. She then went into a bedroom and lost consciousness on a bed. At some point after that, she woke up to find herself being sexually violated by multiple men. She was too chemically impaired to offer any resistance. She couldn't tell us where the house was. She couldn't provide any useful information about the car. She couldn't provide a useful description of the occupants of the car or the men who violated her. She didn't know if she could identify them if she saw them again. She didn't have any bruises or defensive injuries consistent with physical force. The investigation died when no leads, no evidence, no suspects and no corroborating witnesses could be located. All we had was the victim's statement and a tube of semen. If we had located the suspects and they admitted to having sex with her, but claimed it was "consensual", the state would not have prosecuted them in light of the circumstances. Was she raped? Probably. But it was impossible to prove, and it was difficult to have much sympathy for her.

If you ever have consensual sex with a woman and she falsely accuses you of rape, an audio or video recording might be the only thing that can exonerate you. Even if the recording was illegally made and is inadmissible in court, the state is unlikely to prosecute you if they know that your accuser is lying. Could she press charges against you for illegally recording her without her knowledge and consent? Theoretically perhaps. But the recording would have to be introduced as evidence against you, and the victim would have to testify against you. It is unlikely that a woman who falsely accused you of rape would want the recording of her screaming "Oh baby! baby! Harder! Harder!" played to a jury. She certainly wouldn't want to be cross examined by your attorney. The bottom line is that an audio or video recording could save you from a lengthy prison sentence and a ruined life.

DO NOT BE THE BULL IN A BULL FIGHT

Marriage has disturbing similarities to a bull fight, with you being the bull and your wife being the matador. A matador enters the arena, proudly strutting about in a tight-fitting colorful costume. The bull is kept locked in a nearby pen. When the bull is released, the matador antagonizes the bull into getting angry and charging. The matador makes clever moves to dodge the bull. As the bull passes by, the matador thrusts a "banderilla" into the bull. The crowd cheers. The matador antagonizes the bull into charging again and thrusts another banderilla into the bull as he passes. Eventually the matador thrusts a sword into the bull to kill it. The dead animal is dragged from the arena and butchered for food while the matador gets to antagonize and kill another bull. Even if the bull gets lucky and kills the matador, the bull still loses in the end. As describe earlier in this work, women love to antagonize men. Stay alert! Do not put yourself in a position where a woman can antagonize you. If you unexpectedly find yourself in that position and feel yourself becoming annoyed, get out of it immediately. If you don't, you are likely to end up being butchered. Even if the woman is your mother or some other close family relative who you mistakenly believe loves you, get out and stay out.

DO NOT SHARE PERSONAL INFORMATION

Why would you give a woman sensitive information about yourself? You might consider her a non-threat or perhaps even an ally at the moment. But that can change in a heartbeat. As soon as you do something she doesn't like, she will remember everything you ever said to her. She will twist whatever she can to try to blackmail, discredit or embarrass you. I worked a number of cases where women established sexual relationships with gullible men to gain access to their personal information or the personal information of their family members. Once the woman got the information, she gave it or sold it to someone who could make illegal use of the information.

SECURE YOUR BELONGINGS

If you are going to allow a woman into your home, I suggest you get a safe. Make sure your camera system is operational. Keep your money, wallet, identification, personal papers, house keys, car keys, medications, guns, and any other items of value locked up as long as she is in your home. Do not tell her the location or the security features of the safe. Do not leave receipts, bank statements, applications or anything else with account numbers or bank names where she can see it. Do not allow her to use your computer, your telephone, or any other electronic device that stores any of your personal information. Do not borrow or use any of those devices that belong to her. Activity you conduct on her devices might be digitally saved.

DO NOT FINANCIALLY SUPPORT WOMEN

Women like to refer to men as "Pigs." So, what shall we compare women to? Cats. Cat's are generally stupid and unresponsive to attempts to train them. A cat has little affection for anyone who isn't giving it food and shelter. A stray cat that you try to approach will usually run away from you. But pop the lid on a can of cat food and the same cat will come running. Once you feed a stray cat, you can't get rid of it. If you allow it to remain on or about your property, it will piss on your clothes and destroy your furniture. A cat might be pretty, make sweet purring noises, and endearingly rub itself against your leg. But it will also bite or scratch you for no apparent reason when you least expect it. It will whine to go out at night. If you let it out, it will disappear for hours, screw other cats, then come back to your house and eventually deliver the kittens and expect you to take care of them. Cats are lazy and self absorbed. They spend most of their time eating, sleeping, or grooming themselves. Women tend to get cats as pets because they have so much in common with them.

FINAL THOUGHTS

I hope you have found this information helpful. As an homage to my dear departed daddy, I leave you with an essay he wrote in 1960. He was thirty-eight years old and married to my mother for fifteen years. They divorced three years later. When he died in the early nineties, he was a physically, emotionally and financially broken man, almost entirely because he ignored the advice in his own essay. It's an illuminating deterrent.

"GETTING MARRIED? - - DON'T!"
by my "Dad"
1960

I am a bitter American male. Just as saccharin was discovered by accident, I too have made a discovery. It is not as sweet.

Since I hold no degree of higher 1earning, I cannot even bask in the shadow of the learned. Occasionally, the layman makes a discovery that opens his eyes, if not the eyes of the scholars.

The late Doctor Kinsey no doubt knew what I have learned. Doctor Albert Ellis, author of the widely read "Sex Without Guilt", also must be aware of my new discovery. The new knowledge is a by-product, and not obtained through specific research.

As an advertising consultant, I am called upon in many ways. Recently, a client found that one of his needs for the promotion of his product, was a training film. In order to produce this film it was necessary to obtain in a cast of varied talent. Since genuine acting talent and experience was not truly essential, I placed the following ad in the classified section of a large newspaper:

WANTED - - Lady between the ages of 26 and 35 to appear in locally produced film production. Acting ability and experience preferred, but not essential. Write to Box Z12. Include snapshot if available.

This ad ran for seven days. At the end of this one week period, I had received more than one hundred replies. Of the total number, two were from single girls. The remaining more than one hundred replies were from young mothers with time on their hands. Typical of the replies are the following excerpts from letters received.

1 - "My husband travels so I would be available day and night except weekends. My children are old enough to be left alone."

2 - "I don't have any acting experience but I know I have the emotions. Please give me a chance."

3 - "Mother always wanted me to be an actress. I have been in school plays. My husband will baby sit, so I can work any night."

4 - "I am married and have four children. The enclosed snap shots were taken about four years ago. I have put on a little weight since then,

but I put it on in the right places."

College graduates, former professional actresses, housewives-all mothers-all came running! Following the receipt of the individual letters, applications were sent to the most qualified letter writers. One of the questions on the application was: "Is there any type of modeling or acting that you would consider distasteful or prohibitive?" These were some of the answers:

"Not especially"

"What do you mean?"

"You name it, and I'll do it."

One applicant answered this question with "No cheesecake please." This gave me a genuine charge of satisfaction, for here was one honest woman.

I appreciate a well-turned calf as much as the next man. In fact, my wife accuses me of having a too well developed sense of appreciation. My bitterness stems from questions that I cannot answer aloud. I know the answers too well.

What is wrong with the American marriage? Yes, I can stand a loyalty investigation in spite of the fact that I say American marriage. Acting jobs of this nature are not so lucrative that money is the inspiration.

What prompts these mother to reply to a

blind box ad in a newspaper, and reveal their physical dimensions and mental discomforts?

Ask any of the applicants, and they'll reply that their husbands are to blame. Perhaps they are right. The typical American husbands of these women are probably dull, unromantic, excessive drinkers, poor providers, inattentive fathers, and they "don't understand their wives."

These wives believe that this is their chance for glamour, attention, exhibition, titillation, superficial thrills and the other substitutes for adult love in marriage. What an opportunity to prove that they still remain young in heart and body. Unfortunately, they don't realize that they have also remained young in mind.... too young.

Factually, they are suffering from acute infantilism. A husband will look at attractive girls until he is called to the great beyond. This is not a reflection upon the desirable qualities of the wife. This, she does not believe. She must not have any competition. In truth, there is no competition. She rationalizes that she does have competition in order to justify her own flirtatious actions and ensuing infatuations. At this point, she is mentally incapable of evaluating. This playing of games by married couples does more to shake the solidity of marriage than any other single act. If such a wife and mother cannot be reached through reason, the marriage is ended.

Doctors speak of the manifestations of the menopause that are similar to what has been described. Surely all of the mothers answering the ad are not suffering with this natural condition.

Being aware of my lack of qualifications to survey with accuracy, I called upon a psychiatrist, a gynecologist, and a dedicated general practitioner. The psychiatrist quoted Sigmund Freud and the libido was the cause of every emotion. The gynecologist spoke of premature menopause. The general practitioner only smiled. They agreed upon one point; Infantilism. These women cannot adjust to the passing of the years.

They want to remain young in a physical way, so they will be the recipients of wolf-whistles. A typical reaction of this type woman is her constant reference to her age; "I'm thirty-six and I don't mind it at all. I think these gray hairs, I have just a few, are becoming." Children tell lies too.

Another manifestation of this emotionally disturbed attitude toward growing older is the sudden and erroneous realization that she has had a miserable life with her husband, and perhaps they should get a divorce. Still another, is the unfounded cry of a lack of trust in her husband, who she insists is having extramarital affairs when, in all probability, he is being no more than solicitous of her welfare and comfort.

Naturally, the psychiatrist gave the more complex explanation based upon the immature mind and emotions. The gynecologist offered more of the biochemical possibilities for the resulting condition. The general practitioner voiced the layman's answer. He said, "You don't reason with women. If you do, you too will become ill"

These immature women see black as white and white as black. A husband who is sensitive and married to a woman of this type is certainly not one to be envied. My advice for him for his own sake is this; don't reason!

Yes, I am a bitter American male. My discovery is a sad commentary on American marriage. My bitterness is relieved somewhat as I read the letters from the dissatisfied mothers who believe the lies they tell. My relief is based upon one happy fact. I did not receive a letter from my own wife.

I'm afraid to open the next batch of mail.

THE END
Thanks Dad
R.I.P